Brands: Visions and Values

FORTHCOMING TITLES IN THE UKSIP SERIES

PROFIT AND THE ENVIRONMENT: COMMON SENSE OR
CONTRADICTION?
Hilary Stone and John Washington-Smith

DUAL PURPOSE FUNDS
John Newlands

BRITISH FILM FINANCE
Bill Baillieu and John Goodchild

ASSET MANAGEMENT: EQUITIES DEMYSTIFIED
Shanta Acharya

SOCIALLY RESPONSIBLE INVESTMENT: A PRACTICAL GUIDE FOR
PROFESSIONAL INVESTORS
Russell Sparkes

Series Editors: John Goodchild and Clive Callow

Brands

Visions and Values

Edited by
John Goodchild
and
Clive Callow

JOHN WILEY & SONS, LTD
Chichester · New York · Weinheim · Brisbane · Singapore · Toronto

Other Wiley Editorial Offices

John Wiley & Sons, Inc., 605 Third Avenue,
New York, NY 10158-0012, USA

Wiley-VCH Verlag GmbH, Pappelallee 3,
D-69469 Weinheim, Germany

John Wiley & Sons Australia, Ltd, 33 Park Road, Milton,
Queensland 4064, Australia

John Wiley & Sons (Asia) Pte Ltd, 2 Clementi Loop #02-01,
Jin Xing Distripark, Singapore 129809

John Wiley & Sons (Canada) Ltd, 22 Worcester Road,
Rexdale, Ontario M9W 1L1, Canada

Library of Congress Cataloging-in-Publication Data
Brands : visions and values / edited by John Goodchild and Clive Callow.
    p. cm.
  Includes bibliographical references and index.
  ISBN 0-471-49742-8
  1. Brand name products—Valuation—Management. I. Goodchild, John, 1943– II.
Callow, Clive, 1938–

  HD69.B7 B738 2001
  658.8′27—dc21   2001026858

British Library Cataloguing in Publication Data

A catalogue record for this book is available from the British Library

ISBN 0-471-49742-8

Typeset in 11/13pt RotisSerif by Footnote Graphics, Warminster, Wiltshire
Printed and bound in Great Britain by TJ International, Padstow, Cornwall
This book is printed on acid-free paper responsibly manufactured from sustainable forestry, in which at least two trees are planted for each one used for paper production.

*Have regard for your name, since
it will remain for you longer
than a great store of gold*

The Apocrypha
Ecclesiasticus 41:12

Contents

Contents

Preface

This book is the first in a series on contemporary investment themes to be published by John Wiley in association with the United Kingdom Society of Investment Professionals (UKSIP). UKSIP was created on 1 August 2000 from the merger of two bodies, the Institute of Investment Management and Research and the London Society of Investment Professionals, which was established in 1996. The new body is a member of the Association for Investment Management and Research (AIMR), an international organisation with its headquarters in North America.

UKSIP's main activity is the support and promotion of the chartered financial analyst (CFA) qualification which involves the completion of three comprehensive and rigorous examinations over a minimum three-year period. It also holds seminars and workshops on a wide variety of topics as part of the continuing education programme, and it publishes the journal *Professional Investor* (PI).

Most of the authors involved in the Wiley/UKSIP series have contributed to PI and a number are members of the society. We believe that their knowledge and understanding of the chosen subjects will ensure future titles are both informative and stimulating, words that we hope apply to *Brands: Visions and Values.*

John Goodchild
Clive Callow

June 2001

CHAPTER 1

Introduction

John Goodchild and Clive Callow

In March 2000 the former Institute of Investment Management and Research, now UKSIP, held a discussion evening entitled 'Brands: Adding Real Value'. The speakers were Jonathan Knowles, a director of Wolff Olins, the corporate identity and branding specialists, and Ian Wright, head of corporate reporting at PricewaterhouseCoopers.

Over recent years the value of brands as corporate assets has become increasingly recognised by analysts and fund managers. The success of a particular brand, nurtured by a shrewd marketing department, will be reflected both in terms of corporate earnings and share price performance; and in the case of takeovers, brand valuation is often central to the price paid for a company. The meeting last March was held in response to the investment profession's growing interest in the subject.

Jonathan Knowles opened the discussion by explaining the importance of brands in determining business success. He cited the development of Orange, in which Wolff Olins played a significant role. The company was launched in 1994; two years later, when it floated on the stock market, the offer was ten times oversubscribed and the shares began trading at a 20% premium to the offer price of 205p.

While Orange was a runaway success, giving credence to the part played by the brand architect, Jonathan pointed out that an established brand must sustain its strengths via sound management, otherwise it will decline or it may even be acquired. Smarties and Kit-Kat are good examples, or salutary lessons. Owned by Rowntree plc and consistently undermanaged, the whole group was bought by Nestlé Holdings in 1988.

Ian Wright dealt with the tricky question of how to monitor brand values and whether or not they should appear in the balance sheet. He identified the constraints of Accounting Standard FRS 10 (Goodwill and Intangible Assets), and mentioned that, in his experience, analysts had not been demanding more brand information in company reports and accounts. Ian speculated that they might be relying on their contacts within companies to provide the necessary detail. A more probable reason is that analysts have accepted the general reluctance on the part of companies to divulge such information.

The discussion evening was important in highlighting the dilemma facing companies that own valuable brands. Obviously sound internal management and the measurement of brand values are essential to the continuing prosperity of a company, but problems could arise if a company decides to be more explicit about the subject in its report and accounts. In 1988 the London Business School and Interbrand collaborated to produce a 'whole portfolio' valuation of Ranks Hovis McDougall's brands. It was the first of its kind and in the following year the London Stock Exchange endorsed the principle. Subsequently, other companies, including Cadbury Schweppes and Grand Metropolitan, undertook similar valuations.

However, the RHM exercise contained pitfalls. An outside organisation was used to evaluate its brands and possibly focused attention on their value to a potential bidder. In fact, Goodman Fielder Wattie made a hostile approach in the same year, but it was unsuccessful. The board of RHM believed that its shares were undervalued on the stock market and that the valuation would help to boost the share price. Bid rumours continued to circulate and eventually RHM was acquired by Tomkins plc in December 1992.

Clearly few companies are prepared to disclose commercially sensitive information for the benefit of their rivals, and most see brands in this light. The main conclusion to be drawn from the meeting last March was that the new accounting standards represented a small step in the right direction, but further progress was at best a long way off and at worst a pipe dream.

THREE SURVEYS

Finance Directors' Survey 2000

Last spring Rupert Howell, president of the Institute of Practitioners in Advertising (IPA), remarked in the *Financial Times* that 'measuring the value of brands has to become as fundamental as measuring cash flow'. Mr Howell's comments followed the publication of a survey which found that 82% of the finance directors questioned had difficulty in measuring the effectiveness of their companies' marketing efforts; and only 29% considered that, after people, brands were the most important assets a company held (*Finance Directors' Survey 2000*, commissioned by CIAMedialab, published by the IPA in association with KPMG and the Financial Times).

The survey included a joint statement from leading trade bodies and membership organisations for the marketing and communications industries; this called for 'every UK plc to have a board director responsible for marketing'. Only 20% of UK companies currently have a marketing director on their main boards. They also recommended that key marketing metrics should be measured and reviewed at board level, and the results published in the annual report and accounts. And they identified a relationship and communication problem 'right at the heart of business in the UK'. The joint statement went on to point out the need for a board director with marketing responsibility as 'UK companies enter the e-commerce era and discover that in the internet world brands and the effectiveness of their marketing are even more fundamental to success'.

Mr Howell provided an introduction to the survey in which he said that 'finance directors' suspicious attitude towards marketing is holding back the UK economy'. He concluded that 'the results [of the survey] made rather depressing reading'. Few would disagree with that conclusion, although the attitudes reflected are unsurprising. In discussion, analysts and fund managers have often sensed a degree of indifference to marketing on the part of finance directors. The marketing profession may have been at fault in failing to emphasise the importance of brands to the boards of companies; it is thought by certain practitioners that their approach has lacked clarity.

Whatever the past problems, Survey 2000 could provide the springboard for a better understanding of the role of marketing in the corporate sector and, by extension, the value of brands. The recommendations in the joint statement represent a positive approach and it is to be hoped that there will be a positive response. The coming of the internet has revolutionised thinking about brands; it has focused the minds of both analysts and company directors. The next step, somewhat overdue, should be boardroom recognition of the importance of marketing to business performance.

The Interbrand survey

Interbrand's annual study, the Billion Dollar Brand League Table, was published in July 2000. It identified 75 qualifying names; in 1999 there had been 60 companies in the table and among the newcomers were Reuters, the Financial Times and the Wall Street Journal.

What was particularly striking about the survey was the performance of Coca-Cola over the previous 12 months. It retained its number one position with a brand value of $72.5 billion, but this reflected a fall of 13%. Coca-Cola has had a disastrous few years, including a contamination scare in Europe, and the company has now turned to fashion in an attempt to re-establish its former status. Its range of jeans, shorts and sportswear has been successfully introduced in the US and there are plans to launch it in most major European countries during 2001. Brand diversification is notoriously difficult to achieve and some industry commentators have detected signs of panic in the move. Any dilution of Coca-Cola's brand image, built assiduously over a century, could be costly.

Microsoft, on the other hand, consolidated its number two rating in the table, despite the intervention of the US Department of Justice (DoJ) and the somewhat negative publicity surrounding Bill Gates. The company had a brand value of £70.2 billion (+24%) and is likely to overtake Coca-Cola as the world's leading brand in the near future, possibly by the time this book is published. Technology groups (Microsoft, IBM, Intel and Nokia) dominated the top five most valuable brands, followed by the more traditional consumer-brand companies, including General Electric, Ford, Disney, McDonald's and AT&T.

Given the battering suffered by technology and internet shares on Nasdaq and the London stock market in spring 2000, it is ironic that strong internet brands showed the highest growth. Yahoo! (number 38) experienced a 258% advance in brand value, and Amazon.com (number 49) rose by 233%. The technology sector as a whole was the biggest brand value builder during the period, with the majority of the companies in the top 75 achieving double-digit growth in brand value.

Overall the US dominated the table, owning 42 of the leading brands; the UK emerged as the front runner among European countries with a total of 9 brands. To qualify for Interbrand's table, companies had to meet three criteria:

- The brand had to be global and show significant earnings in the main global markets
- It had to be among the leaders in its mainstream sector
- There had to be enough marketing and financial data publicly available to prepare a valuation

The key phrase is 'publicly available', because lack of information led to the exclusion of privately owned companies and non-profit-making brands (brands that do not generate earnings in a traditional manner). Among those excluded were Visa, the BBC and the Red Cross. The main table also omitted portfolio brands such as Procter & Gamble and Unilever on the basis that 'it is difficult, if not impossible, for investors to understand which of the portfolio brands are performing and which are not'; and the purpose of the table has always been to focus on single brands. However, Interbrand did publish a separate table of leading portfolio brands. The valuation method that Interbrand developed in the late 1980s, now widely recognised by auditors, tax authorities and stock exchanges, examines three areas:

- The future earnings the branded company is likely to produce
- The part played by the brand in producing those earnings
- The risk profile of the brand's anticipated earnings

Obviously there is a degree of guesswork involved in the forecasting of future earnings, and the risk calculation cannot allow for the unknown. Interbrand is in favour of showing brand value as a tangible asset in the balance sheet, and the idea has its adherents. The method of calculating that value is one of the hurdles to be negotiated. Interbrand's experience should play a part in any debate on the subject. Meanwhile its league table remains a valuable guide to the changing patterns of brand building in the old economy and the new.

The case for brand value reporting

A call for public companies to publish more information on brand values emerged from a report by Brand Finance. 'The Case for Brand Value Reporting' examines the views of 292 city analysts and 47 investor relations executives of FTSE 350 companies. It found that 78% of analysts and 72% of companies thought public companies should publish more information on brand values. Also 77% of analysts and companies questioned believed that branding will become more important in the next five years. A total of 68% of analysts and companies thought that branding was becoming more important in mergers and acquisitions.

The report measures the performance of individual companies based on the views of equity analysts following those stocks. Skandia (life assurance) achieved the highest score. BMW (automobiles) was rated as having the best corporate brand, and Akzo Nobel (chemicals) had the best annual report. Skandia was rated highest for being focused on shareholder value. While the report revealed analysts' strong demands for better company reporting and particularly for increased marketing and brand value disclosure, analysis of the FTSE 350 accounts showed that fewer companies than last year are reporting brand values in their balance sheet.

Referring to the Brand Finance report, an editorial in the *Professional Investor* ('A Culture of Secrecy', October 2000) stated:

> There has long been a debate about the quantity and quality of information supplied to investors, a debate recently re-ignited by the ability of new technologies to supply real-time information. The argument is that while a culture of secrecy is still the norm, investors will have to base investment decisions

purely on top level statutory information without understanding the dynamics of the market and companies in which they invest.

It added:

Increased disclosure is not the evil many companies believe and that by giving investors additional information, value can be enhanced. Marketing and branding have become key drivers and value enhancers in business. But investors receive little information about their companies' plans, investments and returns in this area.

The report revealed that 73% of City analysts and 72% of companies would like brand values to be disclosed in the annual report. This compares to 53% of analysts in Brand Finance's first study back in 1997. The growth in demand is testament not only to the growing importance of brands and the values they represent but also to an increasing frustration with companies' secretive attitude to disclosure. The survey indicates that new economy and European stocks know how to communicate better in this area than traditional UK blue-chip companies. In comparison to the demand for more information on brand values, Brand Finance claims that in practice only six of the FTSE 350 reported brand values in their balance sheet. It concludes that supply has yet to meet demand.

THE POLITICS OF CHANGE

The late spring and early summer of 2000 were significant in terms of important announcements from leading brand names. Tate & Lyle (T&L) revealed it was dropping Mr Cube, the sugar symbol introduced in 1949 to help fight off nationalisation. A spokesman for the company said that the symbol was now 'obscuring' the Tate & Lyle name. The move was part of a planned overhaul of the company's brands and came after an earlier profits warning. In effect, the rethink will concentrate on developing the group's other brands. Among the possibilities are a new range of sweets based on

7

Lyle's golden syrup and a Tate & Lyle branded ice cream. A plastic sugar container is also being introduced as an alternative to the traditional paper bags.

Whether these sub-brands are successful with consumers remains to be seen, but the indifferent performance of T&L's share price and the City's perception of the company as a dull, single-product business clearly had an effect at boardroom level. At the time of the Mr Cube announcement, the T&L share price languished at 212p, having touched 480p in 1999. The annual results were marginally encouraging, especially news of the sale of its Australian sugar operations for £162 million. The share price has recovered to 285p (June 2001), but the City has yet to be convinced of T&L's ability to reposition itself.

Another pronouncement came from Mercury Asset Management, one of the most famous names in the UK fund management sector. Mercury was acquired by Merrill Lynch in 1998 and had traded as MAM after the takeover. But now MAM had to go, replaced by the 'global-friendly' Merrill Lynch Asset Management. Merrill had undertaken a six-month rebranding exercise before deciding on the change, and one can understand the logic behind the decision. Fund management groups have become increasingly aware of the need for a strong brand name, especially in a global context. The proven value of branding in the retail market has influenced their thinking, and with the continued growth of pension schemes and savings generally, the primacy of a single, immediately identifiable brand is obvious.

MAM was not the first financial name to evaporate. Morgan Grenfell, an equally illustrious name, was absorbed by Deutsche Asset Management and, earlier still, Henderson Investors was bought by AMP. But the Mercury change was made to emphasise the global nature of the Merrill Lynch business and as 'a preparation for the future'. Meanwhile, for other fund management groups, including Goldman Sachs, it is a question of sustaining their brand names. Somewhat belatedly perhaps, they have come to recognise the true value of those names.

Towards the end of May 2000, Marks & Spencer (M&S) announced the first dividend cut in its 74-year history as a public company. The full-year dividend was slashed by 37.5% from 14.4p to 9p per share.

Annual profits fell from £628 million to £557 million and M&S was expected to use the cash saved via the dividend reduction to fund a new-look UK store format and possibly make overseas acquisitions. The results were ahead of most analysts' projections and the share price leapt 18% to 261p.

The optimism, however, was short-lived. Institutional investors continued to sell the shares, pushing the price down to 200p, a ten-year low. Leaked information suggesting a further trading decline over the summer period, particularly clothing sales, didn't help the situation.

The complexity of retail brands, as opposed to product brands, is the central problem. The M&S format, which encompassed selling an expanding range of goods and services to virtually the same type of customer, had its beginnings in the pre-war period. But customers change, as well as society. Anecdotal evidence indicates that many women, normally loyal to M&S clothing, have become frustrated in recent years by the poor choice available in the group's stores; and it does appear that the former management began to lose touch with its customer base during the 1990s.

The radical shake-up, announced by M&S this spring, involving the closure of its European business, the disposal of Brooks Brothers and Kings Super Markets and the sale and lease-back of half its property portfolio, failed to impress most analysts; but the promise of a £2 billion handout to shareholders was enough to push the share price 27p higher to 266p.

The restructuring plans were accompanied by news of poor trading figures for February and March, and the chairman, Luc Vandevelde, stated that 'the recovery of our core business is our number one priority'. That core business is clothing and a return to 'classically stylish clothes' is sensible, if overdue. The group may make up lost ground; in the meantime, M&S has the look of a tarnished brand.

Among the recent rebranding exercises has been bp's $25 million global programme, although this was undertaken from a position of strength. The move to a single brand follows a $120 billion series of mergers and acquisitions which in the space of two years brought together the former British Petroleum, Amoco Corporation, Atlantic Richfield (ARCO) and Burmah Castrol. According to the *Financial*

Times, the Castrol acquisition 'illustrates just how much importance the company is placing on brand image, as the high quality Castrol brand has proved especially popular in emerging high growth markets such as Asia'. The rebranding of its 28,000 retail sites worldwide will be phased in over a four-year period.

So now the company's initials are shown as a softer *bp*, replacing the formerly more strident BP in yellow on a green shield or background. The new symbol depicts a vibrant sunburst of green, white and yellow. Named the Helios mark after the sun god of Ancient Greece, the aim is to exemplify dynamic energy, says bp. This symbol will now be introduced to its 10 million daily customers around the world. The original marble BP motif in the London headquarters of bp was designed by the celebrated architect Sir Edwin Lutyens in the 1920s.

Although bp is probably associated with 'big oil', in the sense that the group covers every branch of international activity, the desired image is now low-key with the word 'oil' being pushed into the background. The bp approach contains an emotional element and also offers something to the environmental lobby. Brands and emotions are strongly linked and the power of a brand emblem can resonate in the mind.

When an Air France Concorde crashed outside Paris in July 2000, it killed 113 people and grounded the world's only supersonic airliner. Egon Ronay, the food critic, was quoted as saying, 'It is a tragedy and a shattering blow if it is the end of Concorde. It is such a prestigious brand and something Britain was known for. It is like losing Rolls-Royce.' Here's how Rod Eddington, BA's chief executive, described the aircraft: 'It's very important to our premium customers and therefore it's disproportionately important to our brand.'

Tracing the background leading to the recognition of brands and their emerging value suggests that the concept was not lost on earlier industrialists and businesses. Probably one of the best-known corporate symbols in the world is the Shell logo, now so familiar on filling-station forecourts across the globe. It was in 1904 that the scallop shell, or pecten, replaced Shell's first logo. With variations and refinements it has remained in use ever since (*A Century in Oil: The Shell Transport and Trading Company 1897–1997*).

Although the new, lower case *bp* is designed to reflect the dynamic nature of the company, the position of Tate & Lyle, Marks & Spencer, and one might add Body Shop and J. Sainsbury, is somewhat different. These are brands that have lost their distinction and impetus in the eyes of the City and the public at large. To rebuild confidence among staff, customers and shareholders, the management needs to revitalise the brand. Signs of success will be rewarded with a re-rating of the share price; failure might attract a predator.

Some groups have been forced to accept the gradual decline of their brands for external reasons. The overwhelming evidence of the harmful effects of smoking has led to diversification by the tobacco companies. Over the last 30 years Philip Morris has acquired Miller Browning, General Foods and Kraft. The Marlboro logo now adorns clothing and other products, as does RJR Nabisco's Camel.

If the brand image remains clear, then this can be a successful strategy. This so-called brand stretching has worked well for such major names as Disney, moving from cartoon films to theme parks, publishing and hotels, and Virgin, originally a record producer and now embracing airlines, a rail franchise and mobile telephones. The essential Disney values of wholesome family entertainment have remained intact; if anything, they may well have been reinforced as the corporation widened its interests. In the case of Virgin, the restless flair of Sir Richard Branson embodies the group: he is Virgin and Virgin is Sir Richard Branson.

But if a company decides to diversify and the new direction leads to confusion in the consumer's mind, then profitability will quickly suffer. A brand name must be clearly preserved in the public's consciousness; if not, there are many alternatives available in today's highly competitive markets.

BRANDS AND THE BALANCE SHEET

Since December 1998 the treatment of brands in UK company balance sheets has been subject to the Accounting Standards Board's directives FRS 10 and FRS 11. Under FRS 10 (Goodwill and Intangible Assets) and FRS 11 (Impairment of Fixed Assets and Goodwill) purchased goodwill and intangible assets must be capitalised and either amortised over their useful economic lives; or where their useful economic lives exceed 20 years, or they are not amortised, their value must be reviewed annually for impairment.

Before these new directives were introduced, UK companies were able to capitalise, amortise or eliminate goodwill against arrears. Although this was acceptable to many UK companies, it did not suit those with valuable brands. FRS 10 requires that capitalised values must be amortised over 'their useful economic lives', but amortisation is not necessary if assets can be shown to have indefinite 'lives'; however, they are subject to annual impairment reviews under FRS 11. In fact, there are two situations where an impairment review has to be conducted:

- When goodwill and intangible assets appear in the balance sheet and are not amortised over 20 years or less
- When there are indications of impairment suggesting that the company's assets may not be fully recoverable; for example, in the case of persistent losses, or if there is a significant fall in an asset's market value

The question of how to treat intangibles in the balance sheet had troubled the minds of accountants for over a decade before the introduction of FRS 10 and FRS 11. Unfortunately, from the viewpoint of analysts and finance directors, the directives do not provide an answer. And the situation is not helped by International Accounting Standard 38, which came into effect on 1 July 1999. IAS 38, like FRS 10, requires all intangibles to be amortised, usually over a 20-year period. Britain and France accept the principle that intangibles can have indefinite 'lives', whereas the US and Japan favour finite 'lives'. Therein lies the problem. In an age of globalisation, an internationally acceptable standard of reporting is desirable.

More generally, and in line with common sense, research suggests that most analysts want greater detail from companies on valuations, regular reviews of those assets and independent assessments. At present, though, the majority of companies do not have processes in place to evaluate those assets; it often comes down to a 'back of the envelope' calculation. Also the tricky question of disclosure arises. Analysts will be familiar with the difficulty when interviewing finance directors: the proverbial brick wall is erected to prevent the disclosure of information that could be of use to a competitor.

FRS 10 demands amortisation and UK companies are faced with accepting the directive or submitting to impairment reviews. To describe impairment reviews as unreliable would be an understatement, especially in the current accounting climate. Amortisation may be seen as the lesser of two evils when one considers that brands are purchased as long-term investments, and the maintenance of those brands is a cost to the profit and loss account. As Sir Adrian Cadbury commented, 'The market value of a company's brands can only be established objectively when their ownership is transferred. Any other form of valuation is by definition subjective.'

On a more specific note, Geoffrey Holmes and Alan Sugden argued in *Interpreting Company Reports and Accounts* (7th edn, 1999) that intangible assets should be included in capital employed at their cost less any subsequent amortisation, e.g. patents, newspaper titles and brand names that have been purchased; but not newspaper titles and brands that have been built up internally. In the June 2000 edition of *Professional Investor*, Alan Sugden reported on the IIMR discussion evening and offered a simplified valuation formula for brands:

Where

> *'Premium Revenue'* = *(Company's selling price of branded article – company's selling price of 'Own label' or Unbranded article)* × *Volume*

Then

> *Brand Value = Premium Revenue – Cost of maintaining Brand's position (advertising, promotions, etc) annually, for the foreseeable future, discounted to n.p.v.*

In other words, Johnnie Walker may have been going strong since 1786, and it may bring in premium revenue of £XXm each year, but if Diageo has to spend at least £XXm per annum on advertising, promotions and point-of-sale to sustain the name, then it ain't no great shakes as a brand.'

For many UK companies, intangible assets now represent the highest proportion of corporate value, and quite often a large percentage of their market capitalisation. However, that corporate value has yet to be assessed in a realistic manner by the accounting profession. FRS 10 and FRS 11 represented a beginning, but they are not a solution in themselves. Further research needs to be done, and the Institute of Chartered Accountants has published 'Inside Out: Reporting on Shareholder Value'. This discussion document emphasises key elements for the company itself to consider, i.e. strategic direction and performance measurement. It also outlines the potential requirements of each individual business within the group, i.e. its position within the market and future trends in that market. If developed, these suggestions could create a model that will help in the next stage of value reporting.

THE COMING OF THE INTERNET

The rapid development of the internet and its implications for business were suddenly realised by stock market speculators in the autumn of 1999. Many private and institutional investors had already seen the potential of the new technology and bought shares soberly; but word spread, and the prices of those companies either directly or indirectly involved rose to extraordinary heights. Rumours of a dotcom interest or an imminent makeover were enough to set pulses racing and prices soaring. Gamblers ignored Sir James Goldsmith's maxim: If you see a bandwagon, it's too late. In fact, the valuations of these companies were based on wildly optimistic forecasts of future earnings rather than level-headed fundamental analysis. And the world's leading stock markets did, for a time, resemble casinos.

The adjustment which occurred in spring 2000, triggered by events on Wall Street, notably panic among investors in Nasdaq-listed stocks, was a reaction to inflated prices, and the catalyst was the US court ruling in favour of the DoJ's antitrust lawsuit against Microsoft. While the sharp downturn in the value of technology shares, including the internet companies, was welcomed as a return to sanity and the basics of sound share evaluation, the markets did appreciate that a new industrial revolution was under way and many of the so-called cyberstocks would undoubtedly survive and grow, eventually producing strong earnings and justifying long-term investment. It may not be fanciful to suggest that the boom in internet stocks resembled the railway mania of the 1840s, when many companies failed but the railway system endured and flourished.

The arrival of the internet and e-commerce means that business will become more competitive but worldwide opportunities will present themselves. Brand names, both large and small, which establish trust among consumers will succeed. There are already signs that a degree of brand loyalty is being built in the internet market and people are going directly to known websites rather than casually surfing the net. Many of these sites will undoubtedly house traditional brand names; Kodak and Sony, for example, have created websites to complement their existing business. This will accelerate in the near future and, given the experience and financial nous of the major companies, they will not allow the internet newcomers to pull away.

The Prudential is a good illustration of early action. The Pru formed a separate company, Egg, to handle its internet business and Egg is now quoted in its own right on the London stock market. The financial services sector has taken a long time to realise the value of brand distinction, but it is beginning to catch up, using simple language and packaging to promote its image.

The expansion of the internet means that large concerns will be competing with small ones. The much vaunted flexibility and innovation of the newcomers will have to be matched if the traditional brand names are to sustain consumer loyalty and profitability. The majors may be better equipped to tackle regulatory problems within the internet system and have the resources to fund the high costs of e-commerce; the minnows could develop and maintain the trust of their users. If this happens then a viable brand name will have been created. Whatever the challenges in this new environment, the consumer is likely to be the winner through greater choice.

IN PARENTHESIS: THE BLAIR WITCH PROJECT

Many brands that we know today will continue to exist during and beyond our lifetime; others will emerge from both the old economy and via the new technology. As shown by the latest Interbrand league table, brand pre-eminence will ebb and flow, and the brands of the future will certainly reflect the growing importance of the internet.

The Blair Witch Project has been called 'the first genuinely internet-driven movie' (Ed Potton and Amber Cowan, *Into the Woods*, Screen Press Books, 2000; this edition was published as a promotion for the *Times* newspaper). Six months before the film was shown to the public its directors, Daniel Myrick and Eduardo Sanchez, launched the official Blair Witch website. They included the history of the myth, interviews with family members and friends, and a fictional diary. Updated weekly, the site scored an extraordinary 50 million hits. Other sites joined in, boosting the hype. In effect, the Blair Witch brand was born.

The film opened in the US in July 1999. The first weekend's takings were an incredible $29.2 million; nine weeks later that figure had risen to $140.5 million, four thousand times the original cost. The success was worldwide and a sequel followed in 2000. Some doubt that the Blair Witch phenomenon will have a profound effect on the way films are made or marketed in the US. But it is certainly true that the imaginative and relatively inexpensive use of the internet saved the producers millions of dollars in more conventional advertising. It may prove to be a one-off, yet it is a fascinating example of how the internet can be used to create a brand image, whatever the product.

CONCLUSION

The growing appreciation of brands as real corporate assets has led to the publication of important studies on the subject. Interbrand, in collaboration with Macmillan Business, have been prominent in this area. The aim of this book is to broaden the debate, and the following essays offer the distinctive views of a practitioner, two accountants and a lawyer. We believe that their individual perspectives will make a valuable contribution to that forum.

Jonathan Knowles's section tackles the question of why brands matter. He argues that brands are important because of their ability to communicate meaning. The development of the information economy may expose a fallacy in traditional business thinking: we consumers have been regarded as rational economic agents, but our impulses and decisions are based on a much wider range of factors, including emotions. The recognition of an emotional logic is significant since any business should aim to create strategies and products that are both intellectually and emotionally compelling to the consumer.

In the discussion on brands and value, the argument is carried forward to demonstrate how companies addressing an emotional rationale for their business are proving more successful in creating value. And, it is inferred, brands should be seen as complementary to other forms of corporate asset, despite the difficulty in quantifying those areas objectively. An analysis of the growing import of intangible assets includes a classification of intangibles, and a basic distinction is drawn between functional and emotive assets. The differences between product, service and corporate brands are outlined, and a branding equation proposed. The issues surrounding the valuation of brands and the role of branding in business strategy are debated.

Jonathan concludes that brands are vital in business because they establish a meaningful connection between manufacturers and their customers as well as employers and their employees. Brands have become valuable assets owing to their manifestation of these relationships. If successful, their ability to build trust and loyalty will result in the consumer selecting a particular brand then continuing to choose it.

A few years ago the phrase 'internet brand' would have been unfamiliar to all but a handful of industry experts. Now, as the internet gains momentum, involving consumers of all ages and backgrounds, the trading of brands on the internet has become almost commonplace. Shonaig Macpherson has pioneered our understanding of the legal implications via numerous articles, lectures and seminars. The clarity of her style has enlightened both the expert and the layperson. In her essay she explains how the internet, by its very existence, has driven a coach and horses through traditional legality. The internet pays no heed to national boundaries while laws are intrinsically territorial. Thus, a website established in the UK, perfectly legally, may be illegal in the country where the user has accessed the site.

Despite the understandable caveat that the internet is not a user-friendly environment – it can be difficult to navigate around – Shonaig concludes that it does not herald the death knell for brands; in fact, it provides the opportunity for the creation of new brand names. But, she warns, consumer loyalty will need to be carefully nurtured.

There have been major developments in the measurement and recording of brands and other intangible assets in the UK. Lucinda Spicer and Caroline Woodward, of PricewaterhouseCoopers, examine the history of accounting practices for intangible assets, current trends and how this area of accounting may evolve in the future.

Although accounting for intangible assets is widely considered as a new concept, Lucinda and Caroline point out that the commercial accounting world has dealt with the most common intangible asset, goodwill, for many decades. Consumer brands leapt to the forefront of the public debate in 1988 when Nestlé acquired Rowntree for more than twice its pre-bid capitalisation. The writers argue that whilst the branded products industry was generating discussion concerning the manner in which the brands were recorded and accounted for, other industries were choosing to capitalise their intangible assets, particularly the newspaper industry.

A major criticism, highlighted by the PwC writers, is the disincentive of the current UK taxation system which does not distinguish between goodwill and other acquired intangible assets. And also under the current rules, the amortisation of acquired tangible assets is not a permitted deduction in arriving at the profits chargeable to corporation tax. This is not a new situation; the tax system has always disallowed such charges. But the Inland Revenue has published a technical note entitled *Reform of the taxation of intellectual property, goodwill and other intangible assets.*

Meanwhile the point is made that brands and other intangible assets accounted for £56 billion of assets in company balance sheets during 1999 compared with £23 billion five years earlier. This is a rapidly changing area of brand valuation, and Lucinda and Caroline provide a fluent explanation of a complex subject.

CHAPTER 2

The Role of Brands in Business

Jonathan Knowles

INTRODUCTION

Why do brands matter? Brands matter because of their ability to communicate meaning. Brands communicate a rich set of messages and allow us to feel that we can relate to the underlying offer, be it a product (such as Coca-Cola), service (such as McKinsey) or even a company (such as GE). The effect of the brand is to give the underlying asset an appeal over and above what can be explained by the functional benefits it offers. Coca-Cola offers not only refreshment, but a promise of 'the real thing'. McKinsey offers not just rigour, but the promise of corporate reassurance. GE offers not just quality products and services, but the promise of 'bringing the good things to life'.

Brands' ability to communicate meaning is important because, as humans, we like to perceive meaning in what we do. Brands allow us to imbue our actions with a sense of added significance. Simple decisions – such as the jeans we wear or the beer we drink – become opportunities for self-expression, for adding a symbolic significance to an otherwise functional decision.

Branding is the process of transforming functional assets into relationship assets. Bill Davidow of Mohr Davidow Ventures, one of the most respected venture capitalists in Silicon Valley, puts it like this: 'You can have people know who you are, but that is not a brand. A brand has to do with a psychological affinity to a product or service. It's something I want to be involved with or own because it's meaningful to me' (*Fast Company*, Jan 2000, p. 121).

This ability to endow a product, service or corporation with an emotional significance over and above its functional value is a substantial source of value creation. According to the 2000 survey by Interbrand, a leading brand consultancy, the aggregate value of the ten most valuable brands in the world now exceeds $434 billion and accounts for close to 20% of the parent companies' total market capitalisation. This makes brands one of the most significant categories of intangible assets and a major contributor to the increasing divergence between the market capitalisation of companies and their underlying book value. The disconnect between the balance sheet and the market capitalisation of companies has reached unprecedented levels: the market-to-book ratio of the S&P 500 averaged around 2 throughout the 1980s (meaning that the net asset value of these companies accounted for around 50% of their market capitalisation). In 1999 the ratio exceeded 6. In other words, the balance sheet now explains less than 20% of the capitalisation of companies, and intangible assets account for the remaining 80% plus.

This chapter explores the reasons behind the rising importance of intangibles, and of brands in particular. It argues that brands provide a key source of differentiation in an environment where the functional differences between products, services and even companies have become marginal. Brands are the solution to what Tom Peters has dubbed 'the blight of sameness'. They allow us to perceive important differences between things that, from a functional perspective, are more or less identical. In doing so, they provide the answer to the question that companies are facing with increasing regularity from their customers, Since I perceive that I can get what you are offering from a number of sources, why should I choose to get it from you? In a word, brands create the basis for relationships.

Types of brand

Branding is well understood and extensively documented at the product level. There is widespread recognition that by creating an emotional augmentation of the product, a brand decommoditises it in the eyes of consumers. In this sense, Coca-Cola is the ultimate brand – it has turned fizzy sugar water into 'the real thing'.

Our understanding of service branding is less well developed. The lack of a physical product in which to anchor the brand, plus the important human component of services, create a much more complex challenge. One indication of this is that, despite the huge importance of the service economy, fully two-thirds of the most valuable brands on Interbrand's list are still product brands.

Although I will cover product and services branding in some detail in this chapter, much of my focus will be on corporate brands. There are two reasons for this, First, because our understanding of corporate brands is significantly less advanced than our understanding of product and service brands; and second, because I believe that corporate brands have a greater potential for value creation.

The advent of the information economy means that an increasing proportion of the value of companies resides in the heads of their employees. Professor Gary Becker, who won the 1992 Nobel Prize for Economics, dramatically illustrated this point when he estimated that the human capital of the US was $140 trillion dollars – three and a half times the value of the $40 trillion of US financial assets at the end of 1999 ('The Promise of the 21st Century', Michael Milken's address to the Cardozo Law School in New York, 10 November 1999). In view of this, the key management challenge for business today is how to unlock the human potential within organisations.

Karen Stephenson, an anthropologist and professor of management at the Anderson Graduate School of Management at UCLA, expressed the issue succinctly, 'Here's the big challenge: Technology without people won't work. People without technology won't scale' (*Fast Company*, Feb 1999, p. 134). Success in the new service- and information-based economy will require a management strategy that actively embraces both technology and a deep understanding of human psychology. Corporate brands have a vital role to play in this process. The ability of a brand to create the basis for a relationship and establish a community of shared purpose represents a key element in creating the type of environment in which the potential of the new economy can be realised.

Emotional logic

I believe that a concept that I term 'emotional logic' lies at the heart of branding. Technology and society may be changing at an accelerating pace but humans are cognitively more or less the same as they have been for the past 25,000 years. We are social beings and we like to derive a sense of meaning and belonging from our actions. Classical economic theory may like to assume that humans are rational economic agents intent on maximising the satisfaction of functional needs, but branding recognises that humans generally make decisions on the basis of three questions not just one:

- Is this what I need?
- How will this make me feel?
- Who am I dealing with?

This perspective means acknowledging the existence of what I call emotional logic. Rational logic answers the first of these three questions, but emotional logic is what answers the other two. Rational logic merely asks whether something makes sense on an intellectual and functional level. Emotional logic is more visceral. It asks, Is this true to me? And it gives our actions psychological coherence.

Le coeur a ses raisons que la Raison ne connait pas 'the heart has reasons that Reason will never know'. Among the most quoted writings of Blaise Pascal, the seventeenth-century French philospher, it is generally taken to mean that the human heart is irrational. I think this is a profound misunderstanding. What Pascal is saying is that the heart has a logic of its own, and it is different from rational logic. It is an expression of the concept of emotional logic.

Scott Bedbury, former director of advertising for Nike and Starbucks, was making a similar point about rational and emotional logic (though he does not use the terms) when he said:

> I'm a firm believer that the bedrock of any great brand is a great product. But that's not enough. At Nike, we chastised anybody who tried to promote the brand solely on the basis of our technology – even though we thought that our technology was the best out there. . . .
>
> God help any company that thinks its product is better,

whiter, brighter, or faster than anyone else's and then just stops there – because plenty of customers just see parity where you might see better performance.

That means that the real branding challenge is to peel back the layers of the customer – to get to his heart, his soul, to a place where he does not even think consciously. (*Fast Company*, Feb 1999, p. 134)

It is a mistake to believe that rational logic and emotional logic are at odds with one another. As Scott Bedbury suggests, the goal is to unite the best functional performance with the best emotional augmentation. This leads to what I consider the single most important equation in branding. Invented by Doug Hamilton, formerly creative director of the brand consultancy Wolff Olins, it says

$$p + p = b$$

Or, in words, a proposition plus a personality equals a brand. Brands communicate with both the rational and emotional dimensions of our decision making. They appeal to both head and heart, and so they provide the basis for a relationship that is intellectually satisfying and emotionally compelling. The mark of a true brand is that it takes us beyond a position of 'I'll buy that' to one of 'I'll buy into that'.

Structure of this chapter

This chapter is organised into five principal sections. The first documents the rising importance of intangibles and describes the four leading types of intangible asset. The second presents brands as 'relationship assets', describes the three primary roles that a brand performs and presents a simple model for branding. The third outlines the process of brand creation and communication. The fourth analyses issues specific to the branding of products and services and corporations. The fifth tackles the key issues in branding currently: the impact of the new economy; risk management; and valuation and measurement.

THE IMPORTANCE OF INTANGIBLES

On 16 September 1997 Microsoft overtook GE to become the most highly capitalised company in the world. It was a symbolic moment – the archetypal company of the new economy overtaking the archetypal company of the old economy. Ideas triumphing over physical assets. The moment when brain finally surpassed brawn. This made for a good story but the truth was somewhat more complex. GE had long been a believer in the service and knowledge economy; that's how it had prolonged its reign as the world's most valuable company long after the service economy had superseded the manufacturing economy as the main engine of economic growth. Indeed GE emphatically regained its position as the world's most valuable company in the wake of the Justice Department's suit against Microsoft, and still holds the number one slot.

Nevertheless, the underlying story is right. There has been a marked shift from a manufacturing economy towards a service and now an information economy. After decades in which the market-to-book ratio of the S&P 500 companies (their total market value divided by their book value) averaged just under 2, the ratio in 1994 passed 3, and in 1999 exceeded 6. This is not peculiar to the US. Research by Citibank and Interbrand Newell & Sorrell, published in late 1999, indicates that the proportion of the market capitalisation of the FTSE 350 represented by tangible assets had declined from 56% in 1988 to 29% in 1998 (*Marketing Week*, 1 October 1998, p. 31).

Baruch Lev, professor of accounting and finance at New York University's Stern School of Business and one of the world experts in the field of intangibles, comments on this increasing divergence between the balance sheet worth of companies and their market capitalisation:

> In the past several decades, there has been a dramatic shift, a transformation, in what economists call the production functions of companies – the major assets that create value and growth. Intangibles are fast becoming substitutes for physical assets. At the same time, there has been complete stagnation in our measurement and reporting systems. I'm not talking only about financial reports and internet investments but also about

internal measurements – accounting and reporting inside companies. These systems all date back more than 500 years.

So here's the situation: we are using a 500-year-old system to make decisions in a complex business environment in which the essential assets that create value have fundamentally changed. ('Knowledge and Shareholder Value', Jan 2000)

Figure 2.1 documents this shift in the type of assets that have formed the basis of value creation over the past thousand years. For literally centuries, wealth creation has been based on the ownership of the physical means of production. During the agrarian period that meant owning land. The value of the land was primarily determined by its proximity to market and the fertility of the soil. Irrigation was the main form of infrastructure.

The Industrial Revolution changed the primary source of wealth generation from agricultural land to manufacturing capacity. Location of the plant and transportation were the key determinants of the value of the plant, and power was the key infrastructure requirement. The Industrial Revolution brought with it the ability to mass-produce goods of a relatively consistent quality and so created the pre-condition for the emergence of some of the world's earliest brands. With the advent of radio and television as broadcast media, the stage was set for the mass economy. It is a startling fact that 29 of the world's 50 top FMCG (fast-moving consumer goods) brands

	Pre 1500	1500–1760	1760–1980	Post 1980
Era	Agrarian	Guild	Industrial	Information
Wealth creator	Land	Craft and trade	Manufacturing	Intellectual property
Infrastructure	Irrigation	Transport	Power	Communication
Holders of power	Barons	Merchants	Industrialists	Knowledge workers

Figure 2.1 *The changing basis of wealth generation*

were launched before 1949 and 13 of these were launched before 1900.

The relentless improvements in manufacturing techniques have largely eliminated the performance and quality variances that used to characterise most manufactured goods, and which provided a basis for differentiation. As a result, producing a quality product is now simply the entry ticket to doing business, not a guarantee of business success. Quality is now generic, which has led the *New York Times* cultural correspondent, Paul Goldberger, to comment, 'While everything may be better, it is also increasingly the same' (Tom Peters, *The Circle of Innovation*, p. 296).

Factors driving intangibles

This convergence of physical and functional quality has led to a decline in the yield that can be earned on many physical assets and explains the reason for the growth in importance of intangible assets. There are, to my mind, four principal forces driving this growth: the commoditisation of quality, the ubiquity of information, social and physical mobility, and the pace of change.

The commoditisation of quality

The last fifty years have seen a massive improvement in the basic quality of products. The widespread adoption of the techniques of total quality management have resulted in a dramatic improvement in the quality and lack of variability of manufactured products. For example, in automobile manufacture, quality has converged to such an extent that the industry-wide average for faults per vehicle in 1996 was better than the performance of the best company in 1989.

In performance terms, the adoption of technologies such as fuel injection and multivalve engines means that the entry-level cars of today outperform the prestige cars of twenty years ago. Analysis by McKinsey shows that a 1995 Plymouth Neon has a faster 0–60 mph acceleration performance than a 1975 Mercedes 450SL, BMW 530i or Lotus Elite (*McKinsey Quarterly*, 1996, no. 4, pp. 65–70).

This fundamental improvement in product performance and quality has blurred the concept of the best choice. There is now so little to choose between products in terms of functionality that our choices are increasingly made on the basis of other, less tangible factors. If you dispute this, try doing a blind comparison of the performance and dimensions of different makes of mid-size cars and see if you can find a compelling reason for choosing one over the other.

The ubiquity of information

A succession of new broadcast technologies – radio, TV, internet – have added the necessary ingredient of mass communication to the mix of mass production and mass distribution permitted by the Industrial Revolution. And now that consumers are better informed, it has largely eradicated any competitive advantage based on lack of awareness about the availability of choice.

The arrival of bots, intelligent shoppers on the internet, is the latest development in this process of increasing consumer information. Consumers now have the opportunity to be better informed about the choices available to them than at any time in history, and to perform direct price comparisons with minimal effort. This widespread availability of information has led to two highly important developments: the emergence of genuine buyer's markets in many areas (exemplified by priceline.com); and the information overload experienced by many consumers.

From a brand perspective, this experience of information overload is important. A 1995 study reported that the average US consumer was exposed to 30,000 pieces of promotional communication every day in the form of advertisements, direct mail, and so on, versus just 560 in 1971. Little wonder that 61% of Americans polled in the 1996 Yankelovitch Monitor survey claimed to be 'overwhelmed by all the information that is available today'. This trend is accelerating: Forrester Research estimates that American consumers in 2004 will have the choice of 200 television channels (versus 4 in 1960), 18,000 magazine titles (versus 4,500 in 1960), and 44 local radio and 2,400 internet radio stations (versus 18 local radio stations in 1960). Faced with this overload, consumers have changed the way in which they make their choices. Increasingly they are looking for ways in which to process information and to simplify their choices.

Social and physical mobility

Greater access to information has led people to question traditional ways of doing things. This has accelerated the social trend, evident since the end of the Second World War, of the erosion of traditional affiliations – such as those of community, family and belief – and the decrease in social rigidities. Mass travel, rapid growth of immigration and increasing labour mobility have produced a society that is fundamentally more socially and physically mobile than ever before.

More than at any time in history, individuals are free to define their own identity and sense of belonging. It is now an act of choice not an accident of birth. What is emerging is a much more fluid society in which people are ready to transfer their loyalties to organisations, even new ones, that they perceive will meet their needs. And they define those needs in more than just functional terms. Research by the Henley Centre (*Marketing Week*, 23 October 1997) asked UK consumers who they trusted, and discovered that Kelloggs, Heinz and Boots enjoyed the trust of over 80% of consumers, far higher than the trust enjoyed by the traditional institutions such as the police (which polled 55%), the Church (25%), Parliament (10%) or the press (7%).

Consumers' willingness to trust a new generation of organisations has caused the erosion of many of the traditional barriers to entry in industries. A good example of this is retail banking. Up to perhaps fifteen years ago, the general consensus was that banking was too complex and too serious to be entrusted to anyone other than the traditional bankers. A recent MORI survey in the UK reveals how fast attitudes have changed. Some 36% of the respondents said that they would be happy to bank with a supermarket; 23% with Microsoft; 19% with BMW; and an amazing 12% with Calvin Klein. Basic business competence is now viewed by consumers as a commodity. Affinity is the differentiator.

The pace of change

Bill Gates is fond of saying, 'Microsoft is always two years away from failure.' He is not talking about the threat of Justice Department action. He is talking about the speed of technological innovation. Recent decades have seen an acceleration of the pace of change. The speed of adoption for new technologies has got faster, and so has their rate of obsolescence.

Recorded music is a good illustration. Consider the increasing speed with which different forms of recorded music have been introduced – vinyl, cassette, CD, minidisc, DVD and now MP3.

In manufacturing, lean production has compressed cycle times for product development. In *The Machine that Changed the World*, based on a comparison of 29 car development projects between 1983 and 1987, the authors report that in the mid 1980s a totally new Japanese car required 1.7 million hours of engineering effort and took 46 months from first design to customer deliveries. The equivalent figures for US and European projects of similar complexity were 3 million hours of engineering effort and 60 months. Even more remarkable than this divergence between manufacturers in the 1980s is that by the mid 1990s best practice across all manufacturers had converged to less than 30 months.

The most astounding driver of the pace of change is now the internet. It seems unbelievable, but among all the new technologies and products showcased at the 1992 World Expo in Seville, *the internet was not even featured*. Now the internet is the single largest source of business change. 'Competing in the Digital Age', a 1999 study by Booz Allen Hamilton and the Economist Intelligence Unit, revealed that executives across a wide variety of industries were unanimous in expecting it to lead to increased competition, with 40% seeing the primary source of competition in the future coming from companies other than their established competitors.

The combined impact of these four factors has been to make the business environment fundamentally more dynamic and volatile than at any time since the Industrial Revolution. To my mind, the new economic environment has three defining characteristics:

- There is overcapacity of production
- The battleground of competitive advantage is one of ideas
- Trust and affinity are decisive factors of choice

Faced with this environment, consumers and employees are asking themselves, Since I perceive that I can get what you are offering from any one of a number of providers, why should I choose to get it from you? And the answer is brand.

Types of intangible asset

The divergence in the accounting worth of companies and their market capitalisation has generated increased interest in research into intangible assets. One of the most prominent of these efforts is the Intangible Research Project set up by the accounting faculty of New York University's Stern School of Business in October 1996. The website `www.stern.nyu.edu/ross/ProjectInt` describes the need for the project in the following terms:

> Accounting systems used inside corporations, as well as the systems of national accounts used in the US and in all industrial countries, were developed for manufacturing economies where most wealth is in the form of property, plant and equipment. These accounting systems were developed to provide accurate and reliable cost-based information about the value of assets used in production, and about the net value (adjusted for depreciation) of the output produced with those assets. But in recent years, cost-based information has grown increasingly useless. Currently, less than half (and possibly as little as one-third or less) of market value of corporate securities can be accounted for by 'hard' assets – property, plant and equipment – valued at cost. Clearly, some of the balance of the value is coming from the difference between the current fair value of these hard assets and their book value. But in many cases, that difference is not great, and it hardly accounts for the tremendous disparity between a firm's book value and its overall market value. The rest of the value must, necessarily, be coming from organizational and human capital, ideas and information, patents, copyrights, brand names, reputational capital, and possibly a whole host of other assets, for which we do not have good rules or techniques for determining and reporting value.

There is currently no standard classification for intangibles. The pioneering work of Leif Edvinsson and Michael Malone put forward two basic classes of intangible asset: human capital and structural capital. Recent research has spawned a series of new categories of intangible asset.

In practice the boundary between types of intangible assets is not completely clear-cut. For example, a customer database is both an intellectual asset (customer information, such as purchase habits and payment records, could be sold to another company with no loss of value to the seller) and a relational asset (assuming that the relationship experience has generated a loyal customer who may repeat purchase or recommend).

Similarly, R&D assets are not as purely intellectual as they might seem on first glance. The inventions and discoveries themselves may be intellectual assets, but the motivation and loyalty of the scientists or programmers that gave rise to them are relational assets. Cynthia O'Donohue, principal information specialist at global drug company Allergan, expresses it simply, 'It's not just the patents, but the human expertise behind them that you want' (quoted in K.G. Rivette and D. Kline, *Harvard Business Review*, Jan/Feb 2000).

The Intangibles Research Project is headed by Baruch Lev, professor of accounting and finance at New York University's Stern School of Business. In an interview that appeared in the January 2000 edition of *Fast Company*, he described his approach to the classification of intangible assets:

It's extremely difficult to come up with a comprehensive definition of intangible assets. I've tried to group them into four categories. First are assets that are associated with product innovation, such as those that come from a company's R&D efforts. Second are assets that are associated with a company's brand, which let a company sell its products or services at a higher price than its competitors. Third are structural assets – not flashy innovations or new inventions but better, smarter, different ways of doing business that can set a company apart from its competitors. And fourth are monopolies: companies that enjoy a franchise or have substantial sunk costs that a competitor would have to match, or companies that have an entry barrier they can use to their advantage.

I have regrouped Professor Lev's four categories to reflect the fact that three are primarily functional in nature (product innovation, structural assets and monopolies) and one is primarily relational (brand). I have also broadened some of the terminology to produce the following four classes: knowledge assets, business system assets, market position assets, and relationship assets.

Knowledge assets

Knowledge assets represent intellectual assets that are generated though knowledge-based R&D (such as in pharmaceutical and software) and practice sharing (such as in the development of management consulting models). They are probably the most valuable of the four classes, not just because of their intrinsic value but because they are generally scalable. A unique solution to a problem is valuable; a unique solution that is easily replicable is exponentially valuable.

Discovery assets are key drivers of the information economy. Whereas the physical economy is an economy of scarcity (a physical asset cannot be used for two different purposes simultaneously), information is what economists term a non-rival asset – it can be used for multiple purposes simultaneously. The R&D cost of creating the software or chemical compound may be extremely high, but the marginal cost of replicating it is close to zero. Indeed, in the case of information, the value of the information often increases, the more widespread it becomes.

The economics of information

Non-scarcity

Information assets are non-rival assets because they can be used for multiple purposes simultaneously. The use of a physical asset in a specific task (e.g. a truck driving from London to Glasgow) prevents its use on other tasks. Information assets, on the other hand, are non-scarce, because they can be deployed simultaneously in multiple tasks. As Baruch Lev notes in his submission to the Brookings Institution (Report to the Brookings Institution, December 1999, Part I), this explains the startling fact that the reservation system of American Airlines (Sabre) accounts for a greater proportion of the market value of AMR (American Airlines' parent) than the entire fleet and other physical assets of the company.

Increasing returns

Physical assets are generally subject to decreasing returns to scale after a certain point, because the complexity in managing a wider span of assets tends to reduce the incremental return to adding another unit. By contrast, information assets generally enjoy increasing returns because knowledge value is cumulative; the second generation of software programs are cheaper to develop and yield larger benefits because of the work done on the first generation.

Network effects

Just as the value of a network increases geometrically with the number of nodes in the network (known as Metcalfe's law), so certain forms of information asset become increasingly valuable the more widespread their adoption (they come to constitute the market standard). At this point, they transition to being a structural asset.

Business system assets
Business systems assets are knowledge assets where the knowledge comes less in the form of specific information and more as a way of doing things. These intangibles are organisational in nature; they represent the value that accrues to Dell through its way of organising its direct-sell business model, or to Wal-Mart through its specific systems for purchasing, marketing and distribution, or even to 3M through its fostering of an innovation culture.

Despite their diffuse nature, business system assets can be protected by patents. Dell has apparently secured 42 issued and pending patents on its innovative business model. These patents cover areas such as its customer-configurable online ordering system and the methods by which this system is integrated into Dell's 'continuous flow' manufacturing, inventory, distribution and customer services operations.

Market position assets
Market position assets are dominant market positions that companies have built up and that represent a significant entry barrier to competitors. They are becoming increasingly common in the new

economy as the impact of network economics generates de facto industry standards (such as the Windows operating system for PCs, Oracle's position in enterprise databases and Cisco's position in network routers). Often it is not so much the inherent product superiority that generates this dominant position as the market's desire to standardise on a single technology.

Relationship assets

Relationship assets are brands. They differ from the other three forms because their nature is relational not intellectual. They derive their value from the ability to create perceived relationships rather than to meet an objective, functional need.

BRANDS AS RELATIONSHIP ASSETS

The ability to create relationships is what gives brands their power and makes them different from other corporate assets. Other assets, tangible or intangible, derive their value from an ability to fulfil objective, functional needs; a brand derives its value from its ability to meet subjective, emotional needs. In this sense, the distinction between tangible and intangible assets is of secondary importance when considering brands. The tangible/intangible axis is useful to describe the continuum for plotting functional assets. For brands, it is more important to consider their sources of differentiation on a functional basis and on an emotional basis (Figure 2.2).

It is Coca-Cola's ability to convince you that Coke is 'the real thing' that creates the majority of the value of the Coca-Cola Corporation, not the excellence of the underlying product nor even the amazing distribution system that Coca-Cola operates. It is Nike's ability to engender a sense of self-belief and 'can do' in the users of its products that explains the strength of its appeal. Viewed with this perspective, it becomes evident that any asset derives its value from two distinct sources – its ability to fulfil a given set of functional needs and its ability to fulfil a set of emotional needs. A brand unites these two dimensions to present a customer with a proposition that appeals on the rational level and the emotional level. As mentioned above, this leads to what I consider the single most important equation in branding:

$$p + p = b$$

Or in words, a proposition plus a personality equals a brand – a unique combination of the offer and how it is presented.

There is a widespread but mistaken perception that brands are purely emotional constructs; that the role of a brand is to incite consumers to behave irrationally by letting their heart rule their head. This is a false perception. Note that, under this equation, the brand comprises both a rational dimension and an emotional dimension. A brand is neither simply a proposition nor just a personality. A proposition without a personality is no more than a commodity. A

Figure 2.2 *Functional and emotional differentiation*

37

personality without a proposition is no more than hot air. A brand has to be compelling at both levels, rational and emotional.

The equation $p + p = b$ has profound implications. It means recognising that, however good your product, it will not succeed until customers realise that it delivers a unique benefit to them *personally*. This means that you absolutely need to define the experience which your product or service aims to give the customer, in terms of what they get, how they feel about it, and who they are dealing with.

Brands have the ability to humanise, and thereby decommoditise, almost any form of corporate assets. The effect of the brand is to give the underlying asset an appeal beyond the functional benefits it offers. Marlboro offers not only a dose of nicotine, but the promise of the frontier; Virgin Atlantic offers not just air travel, but the promise that the holiday begins at the airport; Nestlé offers not just quality products, but the promise of nurturing the world.

Branding is the process of transforming functional assets into relationship assets. The starting point of the branding process is the recognition of the need to supply an emotional logic to supplement the business logic. Branding adopts the viewpoint of the customer. It reassures the customer that their basic functional requirements will be met and then goes on to provide them with the basis for a perceived relationship. This is the psychology of branding – recognising that the value consumers attach to certain things has as much to do with how they make them feel as with the functional benefits they deliver. To become a brand, a product or company needs to go beyond the purely functional and define the emotional basis of the relationship its wishes to establish with its audiences.

The psychology of relationships

The biggest mistake in branding is to assume that the brand is the vehicle for the manufacturer's message. It is not. It is the vehicle for the customer's meaning. Branding is about understanding the relationship that you have with customers. It means recognising the attributes of your product, service or company that resonate for your audiences. It is about *them*, not about you.

The importance of the emotional and psychological dimension is often overlooked in business. Lacking an objective framework for incorporating this dimension into our business model, we ignore it. It is simply easier to work with the assumption that people are rational economic agents. Easier but shortsighted. It overlooks the fact that products, services and companies are always viewed through the filter of human perception.

Scientists frequently express surprise that certain events of low probability capture the public imagination in a way that is completely out of proportion to their statistical significance. BSE (mad cow disease), Three Mile Island, genetically modified crops, and certain forms of cancer, all these events have generated a public response that caught the authorities unawares. This phenomenon is known as the social amplification of risk (Roger Kasperon *et al.*, *Risk Analysis*, Vol. 8, 1988, pp. 177–187). Statistics may quantify the objective risk, but psychology explains the human response.

Branding is the social amplification of benefit. Branding uses these same human mechanisms to accentuate the benefits of certain attributes of products, services and companies. Just as a danger's underlying risks may be small, a brand's attributes may not be that important when measured in a purely objective sense. But this does not prevent them acquiring huge perceived significance. Orange's decision to be the first mobile phone network to bill by the second rather than by the minute achieved a symbolic significance that far outweighed its financial cost to the company, or even the financial benefit to the consumer. Despite the fact that all the networks have now matched the offer of per second billing, Orange's perception as 'the best value for money' still endures.

The importance of perception is often overlooked in business. Companies are run by people schooled in the need to quantify and analyse. They are trained to estimate the probability of events and estimate the magnitude of specific consequences in order to generate an expected value for their actions. But this has left them ill-prepared for a world in which technology and communications have made perception as important as reality.

Consider Shell. The decision to sink the Brent Spar platform in the North Sea may have been the environmentally correct one. Indeed they had consulted a range of experts to validate it. But in the public relations uproar that followed the announcement, it did Shell little good to be able to say so. For millions of ordinary people brought up to respect the command 'Don't chuck litter', it looked as if Shell was doing just that.

By arguing about the narrow specifics of the issue, Shell missed the point. The issue was not just about Brent Spar but rather about the track record of large companies as regards environmental responsibility and accountability to society. Brent Spar was a symbol not a one-off. Shell needed to address the wider unease of consumers, not the particular details of the Brent Spar decision. Shell needed to acknowledge its relationship with consumers, to empathise with their concerns. Instead, Shell insisted that it had done all the proper consultation and infuriated consumers. What they wanted to hear was an acknowledgement that their views mattered. The strength of their reaction had as much, if not more, to do with the violation of the trust they had placed in the Shell brand as it had to do with the rights and wrongs of the environmental decision itself.

The relationship that a brand creates with customers dictates not just what the product should do, but how the company behind it is expected to act. Coca-Cola's response to its bottling problems in Belgium and France during 1999 showed a curious lapse in its appreciation of how its customers relate to Coke as a brand. Coca-Cola was very slow to respond to the initial complaints of product contamination. When it finally did so, its remarks appeared to have been drafted by corporate lawyers keen to ensure that nothing could be interpreted as an admission of guilt.

By confining itself to what were perceived as weasel words, Coca-Cola was effectively saying to its consumers, 'We do not know you.' A much better reaction would have been to acknowledge consumer's concerns and respond with something along these lines:

> We know that you love Coke and all that it stands for. We share your concern that there appears to be a problem with a certain shipment. We are doing everything in our power to restore Coke to a position of total trust for you.

Branding adopts the viewpoint of the customer and sees actions through the filter of their perspective. It understands that the issue is not just what happened but also what it means. It is about the customer's meaning not the manufacturer's message. Customers decide what the brand means and the basis for the relationships it creates. This means addressing both the what and the how. It means ensuring a psychological consistency to the entire experience. And it means paying attention to procedural and distributive justice.

Let me explain. A mistake that men often make is to assume that, if the eventual outcome of a discussion or dispute is fair, all parties will be happy. This is what is known as distributive justice. It overlooks a fact, better known to women than to men, that it is also important that the right process was followed in getting to that outcome. This is procedural justice – the observance of a process that allows everyone involved to feel that their views have been considered. Indeed, in instances of complex decisions and hard trade-offs, it is the observance of procedural justice that is most important to establishing the perceived justice of the final decision.

The role of brands

Let us now turn to the role of brands and the functional and emotional basis for the relationships they establish with customers. I have kept this section at a reasonably broad level, but the next two sections look at the detailed considerations specific to product, service and corporate branding. A brand plays three fundamental roles during a purchase decision: it helps process information, it provides security in purchase, and it provides satisfaction in use.

Processing information

Jack Trout, the branding expert, estimates there are now 40,000 different stock items in the average American supermarket, five times more than ten years ago (*Business Week*, 28 August 2000, p. 236). There are over 200 Tylenol products alone. Faced with this barrage of choice, consumers are looking for something to help them decide between an increasingly bewildering set of alternatives. Brands simplify consumer choice by making certain key attributes the property of certain producers (J&J for baby care, Tide for detergent, Kellogg's for cereal, Volvo for safety), thereby making them the obvious choice in their category.

Security in purchase

It is still a fundamental role of the brand to reassure consumers they are getting a quality product that will meet their needs. This reassurance is particularly important with higher-value consumer purchases. Recent research by McKinsey on the importance of the brand in the purchase decision across a number of product categories revealed a range of 7% to 39% (*McKinsey Quarterly*, 1996, no. 4, pp. 176–178). Not surprisingly, the higher percentage categories were those which involved more complex purchase decisions or higher-value transactions.

Satisfaction in use

If consumers are increasingly coming from the standpoint that similar products or services have essentially similar qualities, the basis for their choice shifts from tangible features to intangible features. Once performance and functionality requirements are met, considerations such as design, prestige and country of origin become relevant factors of choice. It is no longer so much a question of what the product does but how it makes you feel. Brands become a vehicle for self-definition.

A brand model

The multiplicity of communication levels can make branding appear very complex. In one sense it is, but I believe there is a simple model for understanding the core dimensions of brand communication (Figure 2.3). Every brand – corporate, service or product – communicates along three basic axes: what you get, how you feel about what you get, and who it is from.

What you get

The 'what you get' axis is all about the functional benefits the brand offers. It talks about fuel consumption, safety performance, APRs, loyalty schemes, price performance ratios and the like. It talks to the logical left-hand side of the brain. It provides the rationale for the purchase decision in terms of the functionality that will be obtained.

How you feel about what you get

The 'how you feel' is all about the emotional needs the brand can meet. It talks about the peace of mind, the status, the sense of belonging, the feeling of doing the right thing, the perception of

Figure 2.3 *WYG–HYF–WIF model*

personal growth and the like. It talks more to the intuitive right-hand side of the brain. It provides the rationale for the purchase decision in terms of the emotional and psychological needs that will be met.

Who it is from

The 'who it's from' axis is all about the enhancement provided by the company behind the product or service. This enhancement contains a rational component and an emotional component. The rational component is all about the credibility the company lends to its products and services. 'Relax, it's from XYZ' is the message. It's all about competence. The emotional component comes from the additional affinity that consumers feel towards the products and services because they come from XYZ company. It's all about the values of that company.

The result of these three axes is a compelling story as to why this brand is right for you (Figure 2.4). It provides the logical rationale and the emotional rationale for the purchase decision. There are two key points I want to draw out. First, a brand is able to communicate on a number of different levels simultaneously. Second, a brand's meaning is a social phenomenon. You and I both understand what the brand is saying, so brands effectively become a language of their own.

The language of brands

Let us take a moment to see what lies at the heart of some well-known brands. Certain brands have managed to embody certain ideas or viewpoints with which they almost become synonymous:

- Volvo and safety
- BBC and journalistic authority
- Ikea and affordable, urban lifestyle
- German car brands and engineering

Let's examine engineering for a moment. At one level, BMW and Mercedes are all about engineering excellence. BMW is performance focused, Mercedes is reliability focused. Both manufacture truly excellent products. But what gives these two brands their strength

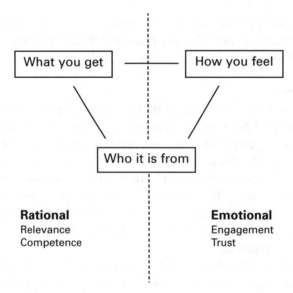

Figure 2.4 *The rational/emotional dimensions of the model*

is the way they have leveraged their functional excellence into emotional turf that they can occupy in the minds of their customers.

BMW has taken physical performance and used it to communicate a form of emotional aggression. BMW is for people on their way somewhere. A product for people who live in life's metaphorical fast lane. BMW is a statement about how far and fast your career is going. Mercedes has taken that powerful reliability and used it to communicate a form of emotional reassurance. Mercedes offers comfort for people who have made it. A product for people who are already at the top. Mercedes is a statement about achievement rewarded.

If BMW is about excitement for people on their way somewhere, and Mercedes is about comfort for those already there, what might Fiat be about? Doug Hamilton, formerly creative director at Wolff Olins, has suggested that the big idea for Fiat might be: We only make red cars. Of course, this is nonsense at one level; Fiat makes cars in all sorts of colours. But on another level, what are Italian cars about if not passion? It does not matter if the car is a Ferrari, Maserati or a Cinquecento, Italian cars are about passion. This is the psychological thread that could give perceived unity to the vast range of cars made by Fiat companies. Fiat have started using the tag line 'Driven by passion'. But that is a pale and pedestrian articulation of the same idea. A bit like IBM saying 'The scale of computing challenges nowadays demands a company with global capabilities' rather than 'Solutions for a small planet'.

American Express is all about status. Is it really? Isn't it rather about insecurity? The American Express card is the perfect prop for those who feel insecure. Insecure about the malevolence of fate, 'Don't leave home without it'; insecure about others recognising how important they are, 'Says more about you than cash ever can'; insecure about not belonging to the right cliques, 'Membership has its privileges'; or even insecure about life passing them by, 'Do more'.

Virgin has developed a potent positioning that combines underdog and consumer champion, best summarised as 'We're on your side against the fat cats'. Virgin has enjoyed its greatest success in industries where a rigid, oligopolistic industry structure had resulted in consumers receiving a really poor deal. Note that the key to Virgin's franchise is the *perceived* existence of fat cats and poor consumer choice, not their actual existence. The soft drinks market is every bit as oligopolistic as airlines or banking, but Virgin has not made headway against Coca-Cola and Pepsi because consumers did not perceive that they were being abused.

Brands become the vehicle for a viewpoint or a certain attitude. This makes them an ideal way of expressing ourselves as individuals. We define and proclaim aspects of our character by the brands we choose: Coke vs. Pepsi; Apple vs. IBM; Nike vs. Adidas; BMW vs. Mercedes; Virgin vs. British Airways. Armed with this understanding of social communication made possible through brands, let's look at some examples of how we use brands to make statements about ourselves:

- I am a high achiever
    Mercedes, Rolex, Hermes
- I am on my way to the top
    BMW, Tag Heuer, Armani
- I am an individual
    Apple, Swatch, Muji
- I am a world citizen
    British Airways, Benetton
- I care about the environment
    Cooperative Bank, Body Shop

The important thing to recognise is that a brand becomes an integral part of the way that people define themselves. It becomes an accepted social language and part of the way in which a group expresses itself. Instead of just marketing to a certain segment, the brand becomes part of the way that segment thinks of itself. The relationship between brands and their message is therefore self-reinforcing. The more they are used for these symbolic purposes, the more they are perceived to add to them.

National advantage in branding

One of the fascinating phenomena in consumer and business environments is the way in which certain nations are perceived to 'own' particular industries, competencies or characteristics. Japan owns consumer electronics, Germany owns engineering prowess, France owns fashion and luxury goods, Spain and Italy own passion, and the US owns information technology, entertainment and mass consumerism. To a degree this perception may correspond to reality, but generally the perception is larger than the reality. Germany's share of global car production is less than 20% and Japan's share of consumer electronics production is only 30%.

National perceptions are often dominated by a single company: Sony is Japan; Mercedes is Germany; Ikea is Sweden; Nokia is Finland, and so on. This phenomenon is a form of mental shorthand by consumers. Faced with an overload of information, national origin is a convenient way to process and categorise information. From a business perspective, this is important because it raises an entry barrier for certain industries. Pity Hugo Boss (from Germany) trying to overcome the preconception of everything German as technical and cold. Even more daunting is the task facing Helmut Lang (from Austria). What is Austria famous for except the waltz, wiener schnitzel and Hitler?

By contrast, the Swiss have benefited hugely from this phenomenon. The traditional virtues of Swissness – precision, discretion and well-being – form the basis of the new Switzerland that is being presented by companies such as Credit Suisse, UBS, Novartis and Zurich. The functional attributes of watchmaking, Swiss army knives and muesli have been leveraged into symbolic values.

This point about the importance of national origin is not widely understood. Open a copy of the *Financial Times* or the *Wall Street Journal* any day and you will find a slew of advertisements from companies proclaiming their globality. Their span of operations may be global but, in perceptual terms, everyone is global from somewhere.

Try to name a company that does not have a clearly national origin. They may be global, but their value set is almost always perceived to be dominated by a single nation. This makes national origin an important consideration in the marketing of companies. The whole Cool Britannia initiative began as a serious attempt to update the image of Britain to better reflect the reality of Britain's economic position. The global competitiveness of Britain in pharmaceuticals, mobile telephony, financial services and creative businesses is lost in the perception of Olde England, a mix of Shakespeare and Jane Austen, Burberrys and bowler hats, with a good dose of industrial unrest thrown in.

Unfortunately, the 'Branding Britain' initiative got sidetracked into an exercise in political spin doctoring. It became too associated with the trendiness of the Labour government and became divorced from the real essence of the British identity. This highlights one of the key issues in branding – authenticity. The brand must be perceived to be leveraging an aspect of a product, service, company or country that is inherently true. Laurie Coots of TBWA/Chiat Day put it well when she said: 'A good product is not enough; consumers today are looking for soul – and soul is one thing you cannot invent. It has to be authentic. It has to be in the company' (*Fast Company*, Feb 1999, p. 134).

BRAND CREATION AND COMMUNICATION

The goal of the branding process is to define a turf that you alone can occupy in the mind of your key audiences. Once done, it seems so obvious. Up front, however, it is hard to know what to focus on. This section outlines the process of brand creation and discusses the dimensions in which the brand can be manifested.

The process of brand creation

There are three basic stages involved in brand creation. Stages 1 and 2 establish the functional and emotional differentiation of the brand. Stage 3 establishes the core elements of how the brand is expressed.

Stage 1

The first stage is to define what is truly distinctive about your offer from a functional viewpoint (e.g. bigger, faster, simpler, safer) and why this represents a benefit to your target consumers. This stage is absolutely fundamental. It is fundamental because consumers are smart; they see through the hype of marketing and can discern when the underlying product has no particular advantage to offer them. It is important not to overclaim on functional differentiation.

The resulting claim should be phrased in terms of 'this is the best choice for XYZ need' as opposed to a blanket claim of 'this is the best'. Nike does not claim to make the best footwear and Benetton never claims that its clothes are better than anyone else's. Such claims would be implausible and, even if true, unlikely to be true indefinitely. However, it is likely that some combination of functionality, added features and service support, combined with a realistic price point, will make your offer 'the best choice for XYZ need'. It is worth being brutally realistic about what this combination is.

Stage 2

Once the bedrock of your differentiation is established, the second stage of brand creation involves defining an appropriate personality for your product or, in the case of corporate branding, the company itself. This involves how the product will fit into people's lives, how the competing products are positioned, and the credibility of the company behind the product. All of these provide the equity out of which the brand's personality can be formed.

In many product and service areas it is literally impossible to achieve meaningful, sustainable differentiation in terms of the 'hard' factors for two basic reasons. First, the product or service feature will be swiftly copied by your competitors. Second, and more important, you will not get sufficient share of mind with your consumers to do so. For many consumers, most products are just so similar, so complex or so dull that feature-based differentiation does not work. Attempts to convince them that some aspect of your offer is better than everyone else's, however true this may be, are likely to go unheard. Only by presenting clearly articulated product benefits and an engaging personality will the brand be able to achieve a unique appeal.

A brand's personality provides a richer source of competitive advantage than any functional feature can. This is true for three main reasons. First, because personality attributes are more difficult for competitors to copy than functional features, personality is a source of sustainable differentiation. Second, because the same brand personality can be used across several different product categories, it enables you to enter new markets that may appear unrelated to your existing business. Virgin's 'I'm on your side against the fat cats' personality spans bank accounts to airlines.

The third advantage that personality conveys is a closer relationship with your customers, because you are recognising that their purchase decisions are made on the basis of both rational and emotional criteria. They want products that do the job *and* that they can relate to. At this point, you should subject your proposed brand to five key questions:

- Is this new?
- Is it true?
- Can we own this space in the minds of our audiences?
- Is it sustainable?
- Is it a call to action?

Is this new?
The basis of any brand is differentiation. You must be seen to offer a unique proposition to the customer. Be sure you know exactly what you are offering.

Is it true?
The brand must be leveraging something that is inherently true. Consumers may be frustratingly inarticulate about the reasons for their decisions, but they are smart. They have a very strong ability to discern whether you are authentic and have the credibility to lay claim to a certain mental space.

Can we own this space in the minds of our audiences?
You may have a differentiated offer that is true, but it may also be as true for someone with deeper pockets than you. Take time to face the reality of who is targeting the same perceptual turf and choose your battles carefully.

Is it sustainable?
Make sure the basis of your brand will outlive the technology cycle of your current business. Xerox has struggled to migrate its offer from 'the copier business' to 'the document company'. Will Dell outlive the PC era? Will British Petroleum ever succeed in becoming Beyond Petroleum?

Is it a call to action?

The brand needs to be action-oriented. There needs to be a clear sense of purpose about how life will be different as a result of espousing this brand. This is where Benetton has gone astray; the link between its brand and consumer action has become altogether too tenuous.

Stage 3

Once you have completed the first two stages, you will have a clear definition of your offer in terms of what it does, how it makes you feel, and who it is from. The third stage involves finding a way of expressing your messages that is both simple and compelling. This is where the magic enters. It is literally impossible to say all these messages simultaneously. Literally impossible, but not laterally. There are three vital points to recognise about the human brain: it works primarily by association; it processes information in parallel, not sequentially; the type of logic followed in each train of thought may be different.

The mind map popularised by Tony Buzan is a very good expression of how the brain works. Each branch of the mind map is internally consistent, but different branches follow different forms of logic (some rational, some emotional, some inferential, some deductive). Since each branch is being explored simultaneously, it is easy to point out apparent inconsistencies in our thought processes, but this overlooks the fact that consistency is a function of the type of logic used in that branch of thought. The *overall* consistency of the decision is a function of multiple forms of logic.

Jean Jacques Rousseau, the eighteenth-century French political theorist and novelist, said 'All of my ideas are logical, it is just that I cannot say everything at the same time.' The huge advantage of a brand is that it facilitates simultaneous communication on a number of levels. Some of this communication is verbal, some is visual. Together they form the 'vocabulary of the brand' so that the core messages can be communicated in the most effective way possible.

Take the example of Goldfish, the UK's fastest-growing credit card for the last four years and now one of the leading cards in the market. The first stage of brand creation had established a core proposition of 'savings on home essentials'; the second stage had defined openness, inclusiveness and challenge as key elements of the brand personality. The third stage involved defining a look and feel for the brand, including the choice of Goldfish as a name.

Why Goldfish? Because goldfish are the perfect symbol for the key messages about the brand. Goldfish are domestic and the brand's proposition is about saving on home essentials; everyone can own goldfish and the brand is about inclusiveness; goldfish bring a splash of colour to a financial world that's predominantly grey. Just as important, their warm colour provides a visual link to the main benefit – money off your gas bill – and a tonal link to the warmth of the home. The surprising name reinforces the message that this card is designed to change your ideas about credit cards: 'You'll be surprised what you can do with a Goldfish.'

Goldfish

Goldfish is the UK's fastest-growing credit card. In a market that now has over 1,500 cards on offer, Goldfish has gone from launch in September 1996 to having one of the largest cardholder bases in the UK. Innovative use of a brand has enabled it to break through the clutter of the market-place, secure a reputation for good value, and achieve a level of loyalty that is unprecedented in the industry.

Background

Goldfish is a joint venture between Centrica and HFC Bank in the UK. In 1996, faced with the forthcoming deregulation of the gas supply market to which it was the monopoly supplier, Centrica (then called British Gas Trading) adopted a strategy for developing into a broad-based retail services company.

Financial services, specifically credit cards, were identified as a potential focus for expansion. Market research showed that while British Gas would be credible as a provider of financial services, the overall feeling about the company was highly negative. Its poor reputation reflected high levels of customer complaint, poor value for money, and controversy over senior management pay.

The decision was made to create a new brand that would be able to establish British Gas as one of the top three credit card issuers in the UK, and provide the platform to offer other financial products. It was a complex challenge: how to shape a compelling product offer for customers in such a crowded market; how to present this offer in a way which would cut through all the noise in the market; how to overcome the negative associations of British Gas but benefit from its positive associations.

The Goldfish brand

The brand challenge was to combine the world of domestic gas supplies – connoting utility, necessity and universality – with the world of credit cards – connoting discretionary spending, luxury and exclusivity. These were very different worlds; could they be combined and could the combination be credible?

A core proposition of 'savings on home essentials' was developed for the brand as a deliberate challenge to the gimmicky offers made by so many other credit cards. This was substantiated by the creation of a loyalty scheme funded at a penny per pound spent (versus the 30 to 40 basis points typically offered by other loyalty schemes). The redemption opportunities were all centred around the home (savings on the gas bill, savings on home furnishings, and so on). By staking its emotional heartland in the home, the brand was able to tap into the positive associations of the British Gas organisation.

The result was a card with an everyday storecard feel – an inclusive, value-for-money proposition that contrasted strongly with the status-conscious, poor underlying value proposition of many other credit cards. Having established the core proposition and feel, the challenge shifted to finding a name and a brand that could communicate this positioning in a highly distinctive way. So it was called Goldfish. Why Goldfish? Because Goldfish triggered the right associations – domestic, warm and friendly, for everybody, a splash of colour in a grey world.

Goldfish was launched on 11 September 1996 and gained huge media coverage. After four weeks the brand achieved the highest levels of consumer awareness ever recorded in the UK. Targets for card applications and approvals were easily hit. Research by the British Bankers' Association in late 1997 found that Goldfish had captured 20% of all new credit cards issued over the previous 12 months and it was the UK's fastest-growing card, with more than 600,000 users. By late 1999 Goldfish had over a million cardholders and an 84% awareness level (only Barclaycard and American Express score higher, and each spends around five times more on marketing than Goldfish). Acquisition costs per cardholder are 70% of the industry average and spend per card is 20% above the industry average.

For mobile phone company Orange, the first stage of the branding process established per second billing as the key product advantage; the second stage defined accessibility, optimism and vision as key components of the brand's personality. And the key to the third stage was adopting the consumer's perspective on mobile phones, not the manufacturer's. This was the key insight. Before the launch of Orange, all the brand messages had focused on mobile technology and functionality instead of consumer benefit. At the heart of the Orange success was a simple insight that phones are as personal as the people who use them. Mobile phones are about the freedom to communicate, not the technology of communication.

The name Orange was chosen because orange is the colour of optimism and the rising sun, underlining an optimistic view of technology and the wirefree future; oranges are everyday items and Orange is about accessibility. The name communicates the simplicity of the offer, and positions the company more as a consumer company than a technology company.

Orange

By July 1993 Hutchison Telecom had invested over a billion dollars to create a state-of-the-art digital network for mobile phones in the UK. But it was fourth to market and it was disdavantaged on the one dimension that everyone agreed to be the most critical – network coverage. It was clear that Hutchison Telecom was going to have to redefine the basis for competition if it was going to be successful.

Market research revealed two important things: first, there was a strong perception that mobile phones were the preserve of yuppies and travelling sales staff; second, there was huge confusion about the differences between providers, and suspicion about add-ons and hidden extras. The confusing and consumer-unfriendly state of the market suggested there was scope for a radical new approach to the marketing of mobile phones.

For a product as personal and potentially so integral to people's daily lives, it was surprising that all of the advertising to date was focused purely on the technology. The brand team were convinced that the secret lay in defining the type of relationship that ordinary people might have with their mobile phone. They came up with four types of brand relationship that could be offered to users.

The manager

This relationship was all about effectiveness and efficiency. It would combine the clarity you expect from American Express, the service you expect from a world-class airline, and the interface you expect from an Apple computer.

The innovator

This was a technology-friendly relationship but one that would make the technology accessible to ordinary consumers. Like a simple CD player, there would be no need to understand how it worked.

It's my life

This relationship was all about customer choice. Like Swatch, it would see phones as a means to express your individuality.

It's my mate

This relationship drew on friendly images of childhood, perhaps a favourite pair of jeans. People never throw them away, no matter how worn they are.

Common elements

Out of these four relationship ideas, three things seemed to resonate:

- *Optimism about technology and the future*
- *Ease of use*
- *Transparent value*

The idea of transparent value led to the decision to charge customers by the second. Up until the launch of Orange, all networks operated on the basis of a minimum 1 minute call charge, plus incremental 30 second charges. Orange launched with the offer of per second billing across all its tarriffs. From a business perspective, this was tantamount to leaving money on the table, but Hutchison Telecom was convinced it was the only way to substantiate its 'transparent value' proposition with a cynical public.

Having established the functional bedrock of the brand – value for money combined with a commitment to bring the new developments in technology to consumers – attention turned to its personality. Five core personality attributes were identified: straightforward, refreshing, dynamic, honest and friendly. The issue was to develop a name capable of communicating them. Hundreds of names were generated and the list reduced to a dozen or so that sounded promising. The ideas of warmth and friendliness had spawned names like Yello, Red Sky and Amber, plus of course Orange. Orange was the name that said it all.

The brand launched on 28 April 1994 and it surpassed all expectations. Within three months Orange had spontaneous awareness of 45%, and by ten months Orange was the best-known brand in telephony in the UK, surpassing all other mobile or fixed-line networks in terms of TV aware-

ness, including BT. In March 1996 Orange was floated on the London and New York stock exchanges and achieved a valuation of $4 billion. The next four years saw Orange win licences in a further nine markets, including Austria, Belgium, Switzerland, Israel and Hong Kong. In March 1999 Orange was bought by Mannesmann for $33 billion, only for Mannesmann itself to be taken over by Vodafone in July of that year. Due to the conflict with Vodafone's existing mobile phone business, Orange had to be divested. In June 2000 Orange was sold to France Télécom for $38 billion.

Adapted from D. Hamilton and K. Kirby, 1999, Paint it Orange, Design Management Journal, Winter, pp. 41–45.

Brand communication

Brand creation has identified the DNA of the brand. Now brand communication must ensure that DNA is faithfully replicated in every brand manifestation. Wally Olins, founder of Wolff Olins, proposed a four-dimensional model for brand expression (Figure 2.5):

- *Product*: the type and style of products and services provided
- *Communication*: how the brand communicates in the various media

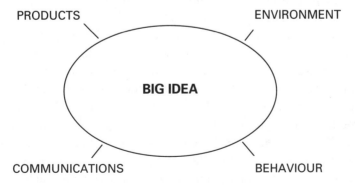

Figure 2.5 *The four manifestations of a brand*

- *Environment*: the type of customer environment created
- *Behaviour*: the way staff and representatives interact with customers

The relative importance of these four dimension will vary according to the type of brand. The product dimension is paramount for product brands; no matter what the advertising says, it is the physical look of a BMW that is the most potent expression of the brand. Communication may be the most important dimension for products that are either too similar or too complex to differentiate on product features. It is Coca-Cola's communication that best expresses the essence of the Coca-Cola brand, rather than the product itself, notwithstanding the attractively shaped bottle and the product's other physical features.

The environmental dimension is particularly important for service businesses like airlines or retail stores. It is the overall experience of shopping at Harrods or flying on Virgin Atlantic that makes the brand distinctive. The behavioural dimension is critical for service businesses. Lacking a tangible product, customers attach enormous importance to how they are treated. The service is a large component of the product. The British Police have resisted carrying guns precisely in order to maintain a balance of approachability and authority that is unique among the world's police forces.

The hallmark of the best brands is that they manage to maintain a consistency of communication across all these dimensions. BMW may be primarily product- and communications-focused, but it uses its showrooms as a powerful expression of the brand's precision and power. The headquarters building is even designed to look like twin cylinders. The best brands are also inventive about how to expand their expression so as to appeal to the senses other than sight. Many brands have explored how to express themselves in sound by creating a signature sound or jingle. The most successful attempts have produced the Apple 'powerchord' and the jingles from Intel and Direct Line. Perfumes, of course, use smell as their signature sense, but car companies artificially use the smell of leather to enhance the perception of their products, and food retailers pump the smell of freshly baked bread into their stores.

PRODUCT, SERVICE AND CORPORATE BRANDS

This section looks at the issues specific to the branding of services, products and corporations. In terms of complexity, the branding issues multiply as the underlying product becomes less tangible and as the number of audiences increases. Product brands lie at the relatively simple end of the scale. They are easy to understand. The product brand has one primary audience, the consumer, and one goal, to enhance the perceived value of the product.

Service brands are more complex for two reasons: first, because it is always harder to brand something you cannot touch; second, because they are delivered by employees. Corporate brands are hardest of all, because the brand has to encompass a much wider range of products and services and it must appeal to multiple audiences.

The role of the brand goes from accentuating one aspect of the product's performance to embedding an idea in the minds of multiple audiences. Let us look in more detail at some of the issues involved.

Product branding

In terms of the four primary dimensions in which the brand can be expressed (product, communications, environment, behaviour), the product and communications dimensions are overwhelmingly the most important for product brands. First, and most obviously, the sheer physicality of the product anchors our perception of how it can be perceived. Volvos look boxy so we are receptive to the idea they are safe. Apple computers look friendly so we are predisposed to think they are easy to use. Tag Heuer watches look rugged so we are predisposed to think they are for people who are fighting their way to the top of the corporate ladder. Second, communications, particularly advertising, plays a huge role in shaping our attitude to the product.

There are two basic approaches to product advertising. The first is to leverage some difference in the functional performance of the product in order to magnify its perceived importance. We are all familiar with the basic approach: This washing powder contains XYZ new ingredient so it is the only one capable of cleaning your clothes and making your life brighter. Sometimes the highlighted difference appears relatively unimportant. Zantac's advantage over Tagamet was no more than the offer of a once daily dosage versus a twice daily dosage for Tagamet. Compared to the medicinal properties they both offered, this might appear a trivial difference, but it was an important user benefit.

The second approach is the creation of an attitudinal overlay to the product, so it becomes a symbol for a certain view of the world or a certain style. The product can then be presented as 'the natural choice of those who. . .'. It becomes a means for people to express their identity: Pepsi to signal you're part of the 'new generation', Body Shop to express your commitment to sustainable development, Swatch if you want a timepiece to match your every mood, and Goldfish to show you've no need for a status symbol. Karl Speak put it well in his article 'Brand Stewardship': 'A brand is a relationship that goes far beyond the purchasing decision or delivery of product satisfaction: it includes an emotional payoff, a sense of security, pride and, in some cases, self-definition' (*Design Management Journal*, Winter 1998).

The best examples of product branding are when some inherent truth about the product, such as BMW's superior engineering, is used to form the anchor of the personality. This gives a perceived authenticity to the brand. In BMW's case they are able to leverage superior engineering to create 'the ultimate driving machine'. Levi's have been able to anchor the ruggedness of their product on the historical fact that it was worn by the workers laying the railroad. The product may not actually be any more rugged than any other, but Levi's are able to own the perception of ruggedness.

Increasingly the basis of brand advertising is rooted in terms of a way of doing things rather than what is actually done. Apple's launch campaign for the iMac focused more on the personality of the product than on its functionality (even though the product benefits were significant). 'To everyone who thinks that computers are too complicated, too costly or too beige' is a classic expression of the Apple philosophy.

The other two dimensions for brand communications (behaviour and environment) are significantly less important in terms of their impact. They can, however, play a very useful reinforcing role to the brand. Nike has used its Niketown retail environments to huge effect.

They are temples to competitive sport, and as such, they are a physical manifestation of the Nike philosophy. And the metallic precision of the BMW showrooms is a powerful expression of the BMW ethos.

Service branding

The branding of services is currently in vogue. Rightly so, given the importance of the service economy. But there is a lot of muddled thinking about what it involves. In particular, there is a mistaken belief that the principles of product branding can be applied directly to services. There are three major aspects that distinguish services from products: intangibility, inseparability of production and consumption, and inconsistency.

Intangibility
The lack of physicality of services was delightfully expressed by E. Gummesson when he defined a service as 'something which can be bought and sold but which you cannot drop on your foot' (*Journal of Services Marketing*, Vol. 1, 1987). Unlike tangible products that can usually be seen, touched, tasted and tested before purchase, services can seldom be tried out in advance. The purchase decision therefore involves a greater degree of uncertainty and requires the establishment of a greater degree of trust.

Inseparability of production and consumption
Services cannot generally be stockpiled in advance. They are produced and consumed in real time. They cannot be recalled if found to be defective. As Professor John M. Rathwell noted, 'Goods are produced, services are performed' (quoted in L. de Chernatony *et al.*, *Journal of Business Research*, Sept 1999).

Inconsistency
The fact that humans are generally instrumental in performing services means that services are subject to all the vagaries of human behaviour. This means that you adapt the notion of quality control to suit a human context. Humans are notoriously bad at performing repetitive tasks consistently. Variety truly is the spice of our lives.

Differentiating services

It is almost impossible to differentiate a service on the basis of its functional features. A service cannot be seen and touched in advance; it is not fully created until it is bought; and it is generally not an identical purchase each time. In this sense, service branding could not be more different from product branding. The experience promised by service brands has an integral human component. This means that the most effective dimensions for establishing a service brand are through staff behaviour and the brand environment.

The inherent differences between airlines are dwarfed by the huge difference in the way that customers are made to feel. After its well-intentioned but ultimately misguided tailfins episode, British Airways would do well to go back to its basic proposition of 'Nanny knows best'. Travellers, and especially business travellers, like British Airways because it takes them back to the nursery. After the rough and tumble of corporate life, they like to get back to an environment in which they are told what to do, and the governess (the flight attendant) takes control.

Virgin Atlantic has a different story and it's about customer empowerment. Just because you are flying, it doesn't mean you have to accept someone else's idea of entertainment. You can choose your own. Virgin Atlantic's greatest achievement is in permitting staff to bring their own personalities to the job. The Virgin Atlantic staff actually look like they are having a good time, probably because they are. Not because their jobs are inherently any more enjoyable than their counterparts' at a hundred other airlines around the world, but because they are encouraged to be themselves at work rather than having to take on the persona of the company they represent.

That is the secret of great service businesses. Virgin Atlantic regard their staff not as an asset whose performance has to be standardised in the name of consistency, but rather as an integral part of the offer in the first place. The consistency that is sought is not some form of industrial absence of variance from the norm, but a consistency that is measured from the viewpoint of the customer. Was the customer satisfied? is a far more important question than, Were 97% of our incoming phone calls answered within three rings? It may be easier to measure phone rings but that doesn't make it the right metric.

Seen in this way, the goal of service branding is to liberate employee behaviour within the confines of a shared understanding about the relationship experience the brand is offering to its customers. Let us consider the role of branding in financial services, one of the largest sectors of the service economy.

Branding of financial services

According to the *Wall Street Journal* (Supplement on world business, 27 September 1999), financial services businesses accounted for 21 of the 100 most valuable publicly quoted companies in the world at the end of June 1999. Financial services may be among the most vibrant service sectors from the perspectives of growth and value creation, but its branding is dismal. According to Interbrand's 2000 survey of the world's most valuable brands (www.interbrand. com) only two of the top sixty belong to financial services companies (Citibank and American Express).

This partly reflects the inherent difficulties of branding services (product brands represent fully two-thirds of the names on Interbrand's list), and part of it derives from the mistaken belief that the principles of product branding can be directly transferred to the branding of services. It is true that both types of brand are focused on the creation of a perceived relationship with the customers. But for product brands the focus of the relationship is centred on the product. In service brands it is focused on the provider of the service, not the services themselves.

Credit Suisse

In January 1997 Credit Suisse, the oldest of Switzerland's leading banks, stirred the world of banking communications with its new identity and global advertising campaign. The force of the message, 'the power for you to do', and the directness of its presentation were unprecedented in the history of communications by international banks. The rebranding was the direct result of two major factors: the changes in the global financial services marketplace and the ambition of Credit Suisse itself.

The rebranding process

Along with industries such as telecommunications, pharmaceuticals and automobiles, banking has become a global industry. The challenge for Credit Suisse was how to be one of the select groups of truly global organisations that span investment and commercial banking, private and retail banking, and asset management. Credit Suisse Group, known before 1996 as CS Holdings, had already made some far-sighted investments in anticipation of increasing internationalisation. Most notably, it was the first European bank to acquire an important US investment bank, having bought First Boston in the 1980s.

It ranked twelfth in the world in terms of market capitalisation, employing more than 50,000 people and operating in more than 100 countries. But it lacked an international profile. To a significant degree, this was due to a complex holding structure under which a number of parts of the group enjoyed separate identities. But it led to a public perception of Credit Suisse as generically 'one of the Swiss banks'.

On 2 July 1996 CS Holdings announced a new group structure to take effect from 1 January 1997. Credit Suisse Group would comprise four branded subsidiary business units: Credit Suisse, the Swiss domestic banking business for corporates and individuals; Credit Suisse Private Banking, responsible for banking services for private investors worldwide; Credit Suisse First Boston, providing investment and corporate banking; and Credit Suisse Asset Management, delivering services for institutional investors worldwide.

This organisational restructuring was matched by a decision to move towards a consistent brand identity. The dimensions of change in perceptions for the new brand were defined as follows:

- *From Swiss to international*
- *From fragmented to unified*
- *From holding company with business units to branded group*

The new brand was built on a number of key attributes. These included both 'hard', rational strengths such as size, capital base, geographic spread and range of products, and also 'soft' features, such as the integrity and modernity of Swiss banking and client relationships, as well as the special culture of Credit Suisse itself, most notably the passion about the value of its work to clients.

The result was the distillation of a compelling positioning idea for the group that was focused on the customer, rather the bank. This positioning idea was 'the power for you to do'.

This basic positioning was modulated for the needs of the four main businesses:

- *Credit Suisse: 'We are where you are going'*
- *Credit Suisse Private Banking: 'Money. And beyond money. Joy of life'*
- *Credit Suisse Asset Management: 'A wise engine and clever machine'*
- *Credit Suisse First Boston: 'Smart power for your corporate possibilities'*

This positioning was then carried through to a distinctive visual style that communicated modernity, but with a distinctly Swiss flavour. Bold, simple use of red and blue characters out of a white background give the group an instantly recognisable visual presence.

Adapted from B. Boylan, 1998, A global brand for a Swiss bank. Design Management Journal, Winter, pp. 20–25.

The focus of the communications effort must be on communicating the personality of the organisation behind the services. It is no small task. There are three factors about financial services that make it a tough environment for branding and increase the perceived commoditisation of what is on offer: it is a low-involvement category, there is a low level of innovation, and distribution is a key component of business success.

Low involvement

Millward Brown (www.millwardbrown.com), a leading market research firm, has an approach to brand equity that categorises the strength of a brand's franchise in terms of a five-level hierarchy (described in detail on page 86). They recently compared the level of consumer interest across three product areas: clothing, coffee and mortgages. In terms of perceived relevance, the clothing category polled 64%, coffee 76% and mortgages 32% (*Journal of Brand Management*, vol. 6, no. 3, p. 299). At the level of bonding, which describes the importance to a person's self-image, clothing polled 21%, coffee 12% and mortgages 3%. In other words, very few people regard who they bank with as a core element of how they define themselves.

Level of innovation

Measured in terms of the percentage of revenue generated by products less than five years old, the levels of product innovation in financial services are very low. Gillette reported that in 1999 40% of its revenue came from products that are less than five years old (www.gillette.com) The equivalent figure for banks and insurance companies is probably less than 5%.

Importance of distribution

Every survey of purchase motivation in financial services underlines the importance of physical (and now virtual) presence in financial services. Given the widespread belief that there is differentiation between providers, convenience is by far and away the most significant determinant of choice. Analyse the strategy of most financial services providers and you will find it focused on four priorities: ensuring the competitiveness of the product, enhancing service delivery through technology, improving service delivery through staff, and upgrading the quality of their physical environments.

Relationships in financial services

In the struggle to overcome the perceived homogeneity of the product offerings, it is easy to forget that what gives the provider their franchise with customers is the promise of a unique relationship. Certainly customers want to know they are receiving a competitive product in a pleasant environment, but ultimately what interests them is who their relationship is with. In this sense, the greatest risk for a financial services provider is a loss of their relevance to customers. In view of this, providers need to address the kind of brand relationship they are offering to their customers. Here are some of them:

- World citizenship
  Citibank, AXA, HSBC, American Express
- Buy American
  Wells Fargo, Bank of America
- Exporting national heroes
  American Express, Merrill Lynch, Credit Suisse, Zurich
- A new way of banking
  Bank 24, b2, Charles Schwab, E-Trade, Egg, Smile, Cahoot
- Trust based
  MLP, M&S, Virgin, Quelle, VW, Tesco, El Corte Ingles

The point is that a customer's perception of the quality and desirability of what they get is heavily influenced by their feelings about the provider. Why else would consumers in the UK display the same levels of frustration after queuing at a bank for only five minutes as they do after queuing at a building society for twenty minutes?

Consumers make favourable judgements about products and services that come from companies they like, even if the functional performance of these products and services is no better than others'. This is creating a prominent role for the corporate brand as the symbol of the overall customer relationship, and it forms the focus of the next section.

Corporate branding

Corporate branding is about defining and expressing an idea that gives coherence to the entirety of the company's operations. The goal is to create a sense of psychological coherence so that investors, staff and customers all feel that they know the company and what it stands for. Virgin's positioning of 'on your side against the fat cats' has allowed it to enter a series of industries that are unrelated in terms of industrial logic. But the emotional logic is plain for all to see; Virgin's strategy is to enter markets where it perceives that consumers are currently being given a raw deal. Diageo defines its idea as 'consumer pleasure through taste' and thereby unites a group of businesses that have huge overlap in terms of customer understanding, but little synergy in terms of production and distribution.

Diageo

Diageo is one of the world's leading consumer products companies and among the UK's twenty largest companies. It was formed in 1997 through the merger of Guinness and Grand Metropolitan. With a portfolio of world-famous food and drinks brands, including Burger King, Pillsbury, Haagen Daz, Guinness, Johnny Walker, Smirnoff, Baileys and a host of other brands, Diageo is a truly global company, marketing its products in over two hundred countries around the world. Diageo is a corporate brand. It does not have a consumer audience (no products are sold by or endorsed by Diageo), and few suppliers deal directly with Diageo. Diageo has two audiences, staff and investors. The goal of the Diageo brand is to get them to buy into the company and what it stands for.

After the announcement of the merger in early 1997, the immediate challenge was to create a sense of shared purpose and unity for a group whose products ranged from frozen pastry to premium alcohol. It was also to underscore the fact that the merged company was not 'the best of Britain on the world stage' but a truly global company that derived less than 10% of its revenue from the UK. Combined with a desire to use the name to help the integration process, this meant it was impossible to maintain either the Guinness or Grand Metropolitan name. This was later underlined by John McGrath, the group chief executive: 'I can't emphasise how important it was that the merged group had a name which represented a new beginning' (Financial Times, 11 November 1998).

At the time of the merger announcement, the public perception was that it would create 'a spirits company with add-ons'. Even internally, the dominant view was that the group represented a holding company with four independently run business units. John McGrath was determined to change this way of thinking. He realised that the ability of the merged company to create substantial shareholder value critically depended on harnessing the combined strengths of the group. He was convinced that the company needed a dramatic reinvention of its self-perception as a truly consumer company.

In the process of choosing a new name, the attitude of the senior management was fundamentally inverted. They had thought of the business as being a food and drinks company, delivering superior shareholder returns through the use of brands, using them to enhance the consumer enjoyment of the products.

By the end of the process, the senior management had reconceived the focus of the business as being the delivery of consumer pleasure through taste. Based on this new perspective, senior management came to see how the group's fundamental idea was to bring the pleasure of taste to consumers around the world. This idea is now celebrated on a large mural in the lobby of Diageo's headquarters in Central London, with the words: We make lips smile.

This led directly to the selection of a name that was capable of expressing the themes of 'pleasure', 'every day' and 'everywhere'. Based on the Latin dies 'day' and the Greek geo 'world', Diageo expresses what the group is all about: Every day, around the world, millions of people enjoy our brands.

By focusing attention on what the businesses had in common, the organisation was able to focus on a shared future and thereby achieve what is publicly acknowledged to have been an extremely smooth merger integration process. The Economist (12 December 1998) commented: 'The merger has worked like a dream. While other mergers have dissolved in *bickering, the integration of GrandMet and Guinness has been remarkably smooth.'*

As advances in technology and communication blur the perceived differences between products and services, it is increasingly the idea of the company that provides the source of the differentiation. Ideas are becoming the battleground for competitive advantage. This makes corporate brands very different in nature from product brands (Figure 2.6). The primacy of intelligence over financial or physical assets is the theme of Gary Hamel's book *Leading the Revolution*; he argues that

> for the first time in history we can work backward from our imagination rather than forward from our past . . . the gap between what can be imagined and what can be accomplished has never been smaller. . . . Technology, especially information technology, is available to all. The question is whether you can apply that technology in a unique way. (p. 10)

Hamel frames the challenge in a cerebral way: Can you do something special? Other business authors such as Daniel Goleman, Arie de Geus and Charles Handy see the issues as more organisational in nature. They ask, Can you stand for something special? This idea of corporate purpose was, to my mind, best expressed by David Packard, co-founder and inspiration of Hewlett Packard, when he said:

> As we investigate [the real reason for our being], we inevitably come to the conclusion that a group of people get together and exist as an organisation that we call a company, so that they are able to accomplish something collectively that they could not accomplish separately – they make a contribution to society, a phrase which sounds trite but is fundamental. (Quoted in Charles Handy, *The Hungry Spirit*, p. 77.)

This perspective suggests that the foundation of a company is its ability to create and sustain relationships with its employees and

Dimension	Product brands	Corporate brands
Audience	Consumers	Multiple
Role	Incite to buy	Invite to buy into
Purpose	Leverage some functional difference	Communicate core values
Emotion	Desire	Belief
Brand guardian	Product manager	Chief executive
Primary focus	External	Internal

Figure 2.6 *Key differences between corporate brands and product brands*

customers based on a shared ambition – the company then becomes a 'purposeful community'. In many ways, this is common sense. The fact that the companies comprise human beings whose search for meaning and purpose is often played out extensively in the work environment means that companies must pay great heed to the non-financial aspirations they are seeking to fulfil in their workplaces.

In their book *Built to Last*, Collins and Porras relate how they set out to research what made truly exceptional companies different from their key competitors. They adopted a novel approach to their research by studying pairs of companies and choosing comparison companies that were excellent in their own right. Their goal was to isolate the timeless principles of management that distinguish outstanding companies.

In reading it, one can sense their frustration that the answer did not prove to be a combination of hard, quantitative management skills but rather an amalgam of soft capabilities. The key components of enduring business success appeared to be a sense of purpose, a set of shared beliefs, and the desire to be a part of something whose value could not be expressed simply in financial terms.

Their research caused them to shift their perspective in a fundamental way; they went from seeing companies as the vehicle for getting products on the market to seeing products as the vehicle for the ongoing existence of companies. In other words, the company becomes the embodiment of an idea, and each generation of products are the expression of that idea at a specific point in time. In this sense, the greatest creation of the company is the company itself and the goal of leadership is to nurture the sense of community and purpose that makes that company unique. The primary role of 'visionary leaders', as Collins and Porras termed them, is to concentrate first on the organisation's systems and values, and only then on its products.

Seen in this light, the traditional engineering-based metaphor for business appears outdated. Companies are not machines, and humans cannot be seen as simple inputs to the production function. The command and control style of management, so popular since the Industrial Revolution, is poorly suited to the new, dynamic environment. A biology-based metaphor is more appropriate for the new environment. Companies can be seen as biological organisms, and it is the glue of a shared idea that provides the continuity of purpose. Charles Handy expressed this notion of a community in his 1995 book *Beyond Certainty*:

> It will be more difficult to hold organisations and societies together. The softer words of leadership and vision will replace the tougher words of control and authority because the tough words won't bite any more. Organisations will have to become communities rather than properties, with members not employees. (p. 7)

He developed this idea further in his 1997 book *The Hungry Spirit*:

> The successful company will try to ensure that its soul and its personality or essence outlive the transient careers of its people. . . .
> 'Soul' is one of those concepts that, like beauty, evaporates when you try to define it, but like beauty is instantly recognisable when you meet it. Organisations have a feel about them, a feel which the visitor picks up as soon as he or she enters the building or, more often, merely encounters one of the people

who work there. There is an abundance of what can best be called the 'E' factors, when 'E' stands for energy, enthusiasm, effort, excitement, excellence and so on. More than that, the talk is about 'we', not 'I', and there is a sense that the organisation is on some sort of crusade, not just to make money, but something grander, something worthy of one's commitment, skills and time. (p. 158)

This notion of the company as a community is developed further in *The Big Idea*. There Robert Jones argues for the importance of companies to define a big idea that can form the basis of a 'purposeful community' in which the loyalty of employees and customers is achieved through a shared belief system. He makes the important point that although the idea may initially be defined by the management of the company, it swiftly becomes shared by each member. It becomes internalised by the various stakeholders.

All of these ideas express for me the important role performed by a corporate brand. The idea for the company becomes embodied in the brand and provides a sense of psychological and emotional unity to what may, at a functional level, be a disparate set of activities. The brand becomes the vehicle for meaning. In terms of system dynamics, this makes the corporate brand a property of the overall system, not just an element. In his book *The Web of Life*, Fritjof Capra describes this important concept of systemic properties:

The great shock of twentieth century science has been that systems cannot be understood by analysis. The properties of the parts are not intrinsic properties, but can be understood only within the context of the greater whole. . . . Accordingly, systems thinking does not concentrate on basic building blocks but rather on basic principles of organisation. . . . Systemic properties are destroyed when a system is dissected into isolated elements. . . . In the study of structure we measure and weigh things. Patterns, however, cannot be measured and weighed: they must be mapped. To understand a pattern, we must map the configuration of relationships.

In this sense the corporate brand is the psychological pattern which defines that particular system or company. It serves to define and communicate the nature and basis of the relationships which form the 'purpose community' that a company represents.

ISSUES IN BRANDING

This section addresses three of the most important issues in branding currently: the impact of the new economy; risk management; brand valuation and measurement.

Brands and the new economy

There is a lot of hype and confusion about the new economy and what it means for brands. At one extreme, it is seen as heralding the death of branding. At the other, it is seen as ushering in of the golden age of branding. Both schools of thought have elements of truth. The 'death of brands' school points to the existence of bots and says that now consumers can do like-for-like comparisons on the functionality of different offers as well as direct price comparisons, the role of the brand in providing security of purchase is now largely obsolete. Proponents for the golden age of branding base their optimism on the fact that, for the first time ever, there can be genuine one-to-one marketing with consumers, thanks to high-speed connectivity and the existence of applications that allow analysis of consumers' clickstreams in real time.

As ever, reality is rather more complex and fluid than either of these extremes suggest. My perspective on the new economy and the internet is as follows: in terms of its impact on business, the internet is quite simply the most significant business development since the Industrial Revolution. It has catapulted us into the Information Economy and fundamentally changed a number of the traditional rules for doing business. In particular, it has created an environment in which access to ideas and information forms the driver of competitive advantage rather than access to physical production; it has moved us from the economics of scarcity (where the means of production are rival assets) to the economics of abundance; it has brought about the 'death of distance' and the demise of natural local monopolies; and it has dramatically reduced many of the traditional costs of doing business, thereby creating the opportunity for a new generation of business models.

But in branding terms, the picture is paradoxical. On the one hand, as a communications technology, the internet is as revolutionary as the printing press or the television. These technologies created the basis for one-to-many communication. The internet creates the basis for one-to-one communication on a mass basis. On the other hand, in human terms, the internet is simply one more channel through which the brand relationship must be expressed.

There are two common mistakes to avoid concerning the internet. The first is to view it as the latest and most cost-effective of the one-to-many broadcast media. The real significance of the internet is its ability to make personal, interactive communication possible with multiple audiences simultaneously. The second is to view the internet as a stand-alone medium for communicating with customers. For the vast majority of businesses, the internet will become an important and maybe even the principal channel for communicating with customers, but it will not represent the only channel of communication. Customers will base their view of their brand relationship on the total experience of the brand *not* just the experience of the website.

Technology changes but humans remain the same

The heart of the paradox is that the internet may be new, but our needs as humans are old. New technologies enable our basic needs to be met in new and often surprising ways. It changes the basis of the relationships we have with existing companies and creates the opportunity for new relationships (such as with ISPs and portals) but it does not replace the need for relationships. The internet may be the pure arm's-length medium but most of us still want to feel that we have relationships via the internet, rather than just transactional experiences.

The new technology may make possible a whole range of novel applications and features, but just because they are possible does not necessarily mean they are valued by consumers. Bots are a classic example of this phenomenon; their current low penetration of online shopping is taken by many as a sign that consumers are 'irrational' in failing to choose the value-maximising method of shopping. But this overlooks the fact that consumers are looking for multiple needs to be met, and the lowest price is only one of them.

Some feel that the speed of technological change is the largest challenge in business today. I would argue that forecasting the speed of technology *adoption* is the hardest thing in business. Overcoming a technical challenge is one thing; convincing customers to adopt the new way of doing things is another. Look at automatic tellers (ATMs) and phone/internet banking. In technical terms, they are manifestly win-win solutions for the bank and the customer. But their rate of adoption has been slow, for perfectly understandable human reasons. Always remember that human decisions include a strong component of consumer psychology and ergonomics. The PC only took off when IBM entered the market to legitimise it; the PDA (personal digital assistant) market only took off when Palm made functionality subordinate to pocket size in designing the Palm Pilot.

The role of the brand is to provide the psychological context in which the new technology can be seen as providing the basis for an evolution of an existing relationship, or to form the basis of a new relationship.

Few areas of the new economy have been the focus of so much technical and marketing investment as online banking, but with so little to show for it. Despite the huge investment, so far only 7% of all banking customers over age 16 have online bank accounts. Part of this is explained by the low-involvement nature of banking. Mitchell Caplan, chief banking officer at E-Trade Group, puts it this way: 'Online banking is like a root canal. You can try to make it more interesting, more economic, but it's just not as interesting as, say, online investing toward your future' (*Fast Company*, July 2000, p. 142). But part of it is also explained by the fact that most customers are looking for a total package, not a channel-specific solution.

It is interesting that one of the most successful online banks in the US is Wells Fargo. Interesting because they have a brand that actively supports the idea of new technologies and innovation. For more than 150 years Wells Fargo's icon has been the stagecoach and they have actively fostered its meaning to go beyond its Gold Rush roots and stand for the bank's willingness to blaze a trail into new frontiers. Wells Fargo currently has close to 2 million online account holders and is adding 110,000 new customers every month. At 14%

it ranks top of all the major banks in terms of the percentage of online banking customers. Bank of America comes a distant second with a 9.6% share.

Does the brand explain Wells Fargo's online success? No. Does it mean that the bank's active efforts to encourage its clientele to start using remote forms of banking were seen by consumers as consistent with their brand relationship? Absolutely. In brand terms, familiarity breeds content. Humans like consistency. It helps them know where they stand, and know what they can expect. The brand caters to this sense of expectation on the part of its audiences. This means brands are also vulnerable when those expectations are not met.

Risk management for brands

Brands are some of the most valuable forms of corporate asset, but also the most vulnerable. The brand's role as the symbol of the relationship between a customer and a provider means it is affected by the failure to deliver on any aspect of that relationship, even when that failure is not the direct responsibility of the brand owner. Protection of a brand is not primarily an issue of contingency planning; it is about active management of the brand relationship. The most significant risk for a brand is the gradual degradation of the day-to-day quality of the brand experience rather than specific event risk. Instead of asking how to respond when things go wrong, always try to ask, What should things be like when everything is fine?

One of the most frequent causes of failure to sustain a brand is the belief that it is the underlying product or service alone that provides its unique appeal. Managers believe that everything is fine so long as the product's performance conforms to specification and the phones are answered within three rings. But this overlooks the fact that human decisions are generally based on a mix of rational and emotional considerations. Branding involves paying as much attention to the sources of emotional uniqueness as it does to the sources of functional uniqueness.

What are the risks to a brand?
Simply put, the risk to a brand is anything that upsets the perceived relationship with customers. Failure to deliver against expectations

77

is tantamount to a broken promise. It undermines the trust that lies at the heart of each brand. This failure has to be understood more widely than the simple failure to deliver on the functional aspects of the relationship. The most visible way to undermine a brand is to fail to deliver on the basic functional promise, but it is frequently the failure to fulfil the emotional dimension of the brand that leads to the most permanent source of damage to a brand.

The force of the public response to Shell's decision to dispose of the Brent Spar oil rig in the North Sea had at least as much to do with the perceived violation of consumer trust as it had to do with the rights and wrongs of the environmental decision itself. And Coca-Cola's insensitive handling of its bottling problems in Belgium and France turned an unfortunate industrial malfunction into a consumer relations nightmare.

Intel fell into the same trap when the original Pentium chip was discovered to have a design fault that caused a miscalculation. Intel was, of course, strictly correct in pointing to the extreme statistical improbability (something like 1 in 10 billion) that the defect would have any material consequence. They missed the point. People thought of Intel as providing products of the highest quality. To hear Intel say, 'Okay, so our product is not quite as perfect as it should be, but hey, what difference will that make?' was a slap in the face for users who had hitherto given Intel products their total trust.

The power of a brand lies in the uniqueness of the perceived relationship. The key challenge is to understand the precise nature of that relationship to identify the risks of it being compromised.

Maintaining functional integrity

Sabotage
Deliberate sabotage of consumer products is fortunately rare (such as adding ground glass to J&J's baby food, lacing Mars bars with rat poison, or spiking Tylenol with poison).

Dishonesty
Simple dishonesty and inadequate controls lay behind Nick Leeson's ability to bankrupt Barings, or Sumitomo to incur huge losses on copper trades. Many thousands of pensioners in the UK are also

suffering the consequences of the failure to adequately police Robert Maxwell's dealings.

Event risk

Sometimes the integrity of a product or service is compromised through 'acts of God' beyond the control of the company. Examples might be the outages for internet firms, manufacturing system failures such as Perrier's benzene problem, or Coke's recent carbon dioxide contamination.

Employee or contractor negligence

The most notorious examples of negligence are the oil tankers *Amoco Cadiz* and *Exxon Valdez*, where the negligence of subcontractors caused huge damage to the reputation of the companies that operated them. The tenth anniversary of the *Exxon Valdez* shipwreck showed how these memories are slow to fade.

Product failure

Occasionally a company fails to subject its products to sufficiently rigorous assessment and releases a substandard item onto the market. The Mercedes A Class tipped over during its cones test, and Intel's original Pentium chip suffered a malfunction.

Maintaining emotional integrity

Vulnerability to promotion

Pepsi's sponsorship of Michael Jackson's tour was a source of embarrassment to the company when Michael Jackson was publicly accused of child molesting.

Misjudging the mood of consumers or staff

BA has been plagued over recent years by its failure to match the internal reality of the BA brand with its aspirational external image. Staff experienced a huge disconnect between the external communications and their treatment by the company. Similarly, Shell's belief that its actions in Nigeria and with Brent Spar were not matters of public interest represented a huge miscalculation about the feelings of consumers.

Empty promises

Nowhere is it harder to ensure the consistency of the brand experience than in service industries. This is due to the inherent difficulties in standardising anything which involves a human component. Lacking a physical product to anchor perceptions of the brand, the tendency is to make grandiose promises. Few of these promises are kept in practice.

What can be done to protect brands?

Some of the risks can be reduced by having proper control systems; some can be reduced by adequate training for staff and anyone else who has an important role in delivering the brand experience; and some can be reduced by a more pronounced emphasis on corporate culture. Risk reduction may be about prevention, through control systems; about articulation of desired behaviours; or about developing a concept of the brand as a 'way of being' for the company.

The essence of the challenge is to maintain whatever it is that gives the brand its unique appeal. Delivering on that promise requires guarding against two principal threats: inconsistency and commoditisation. Inconsistency is a failure to deliver an identical experience time and again, or across different media. Consistency is hard enough to achieve in a product environment, and it is harder still in a service environment. Commoditisation is the risk that the unique appeal of the product or service will be lost, either due to its widespread familiarity or because it is copied by competitors. I have not covered the legal issues of infringement by third parties; see Chapter 4.

The secret of combating these two threats lies in defining the brand's promise to consumers, ensuring this promise is met at every consumer encounter, and assiduously defending the legal right to the brand 'cues' that represent it in the minds of consumers.

Brand valuation and measurement

If the importance of brands is no longer in dispute, devising a methodology for measuring them has proved elusive. Brand measurement methodologies come in two basic flavours: those designed to establish the financial value of a brand, and those designed to analyse the basic strength of a brand in terms of the degree of consumer loyalty it commands.

Brand valuation

Brand valuation is a very young discipline. Interbrand, a brand consultancy, conducted its first brand valuation survey for Ranks Hovis McDougall in 1988, as part of RHM's defence against a hostile takeover from Goodman Fielder Wattie. Most brand valuation approaches use discounted cash flow (DCF) to value the incremental income the brand generates over and above the income for an equivalent, unbranded product. The best known of the early practitioners was the US financial magazine *Financial World* (now defunct), which estimated brand values based on a multiple of historic brand earnings. In essence this involved two steps: identifying the earnings uniquely attributable to the brand by deducting from the earnings of the branded products what were the equivalent earnings of a generic competitor; and determining the appropriate multiple to apply based on the brand's strength.

Later methodologies have adopted a DCF approach to the valuation of future brand earnings. These typically involve developing a 5–10 year forecast of the earnings attributable to the brand, and then adding a terminal value, or annuity, to cover the brand's earnings beyond the forecast period. The second stage of the process is to determine the appropriate discount rate to be applied to the brand earnings based on the perceived robustness of the revenue stream. Figure 2.7 shows the approach of Brand Finance, a UK brand consultancy. The methodologies of different practitioners vary in their details, but the DCF approach has been endorsed by the Accounting Standards Board in Financial Reporting Standard 10 as the appropriate way of valuing intangibles on the balance sheet.

More recently a number of practitioners have tried to use option pricing theory for the valuation of brands. This approach values brands not on the basis of a single central forecast (the DCF approach) but on the spread of likely outcomes given certain key variables. Although this is conceptually the most accurate approach to brand valuation, it is also the most difficult to understand and therefore the least likely to achieve client reassurance, let alone client buy-in.

Brand measurement

Brand measurement is a market research approach; it analyses the strength of a brand along the dimensions that are most salient for consumers. There are several competing methodologies in the market; two of the more robust are the Brand Asset Valuator from Young & Rubicam (Y&R) and BrandDynamics from Millward Brown.

The Brand Asset Valuator

According to Young & Rubicam's website, the Brand Asset Valuator (BAV) is based on over 90,000 customer interviews across 30 countries. Information on more than 13,000 brands has been collected, providing up to 50 different dimensions of consumer perception.

The basis of the BAV is Y&R's hypothesis that there is a specific progression in the development of brands that remains true, irrespective of product categories. When building a brand, differentiation comes first. Differentiation measures the strength of the brand's meaning. Next comes relevance. Relevance measures the personal appropriateness of a brand to consumers. The third and fourth dimensions are esteem and knowledge. Esteem measures the level of regard for the brand, based principally on perceptions of quality and

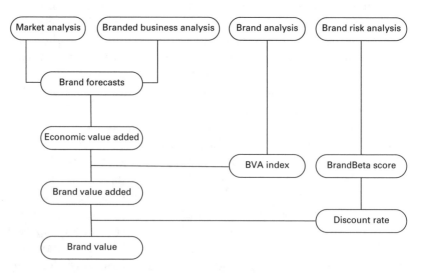

Figure 2.7 *Brand Finance chart's methodology for brand valuation*

popularity. Knowledge measures being aware of the brand and knowing what the brand stands for.

A standardised profile of a brand can be built based on these four dimensions. The Y&R website (`www.yr.com/bav`) contains a useful interpretation of the different profiles, such as unrealised potential (very high differentiation, high relevance, medium esteem, low knowledge) or exotic/prestige (very high differentiation and esteem, low relevance and knowledge), and commodity (very high relevance and knowledge, but low differentiation and esteem).

Y&R combine the differentiation and relevance to form a single score for brand strength, and they combine esteem and knowledge to form a single score for brand stature. The two dimensions of brand strength and brand stature are then used as the axes of their Power Grid. Y&R suggest there is a natural progression through the quadrants of the Power Grid from new entrant to unrealised potential to leadership to eroding (Figure 2.8).

Interestingly, Y&R have tried to correlate the BAV with the financial performance of brands. Y&R have calculated the mean earnings growth and margin for three of the four quadrants and report that earnings growth and margins are highest in the high brand strength/low brand stature quadrant when the brand is growing most rapidly (Figure 2.9).

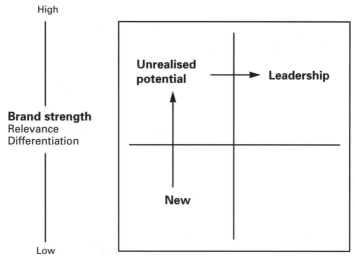

Figure 2.8 *The natural progression of a brand*

BrandDynamics

Millward Brown's literature claims that the BrandDynamics model has monitored over 10,000 brands in over 35 countries. It puts forward a pyramid approach to brand equity, consisting of five levels. At the base of the pyramid is presence, which is established through unaided awareness, remembered trial, or understanding of the brand promise. The second level is relevance, Is the product capable of meeting the consumer's criteria for choice? The third level is performance, Is the product performance acceptable? The fourth level is advantage, Does the product offer a distinctive positioning? The top level is bonding, Do consumers claim that this brand is the only one capable of fulfilling their requirements? (Figure 2.10)

These research methodologies are well suited to the assessment of product brands, where the level of transactions makes the measurements relatively simple albeit time-consuming. An altogether more

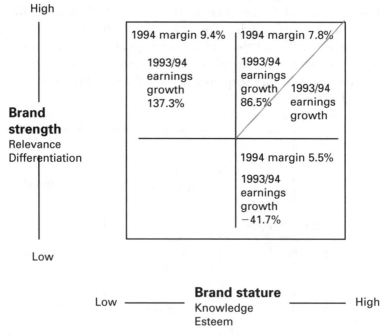

Figure 2.9 *Growth and margins by Power Grid quadrant*

daunting challenge is to establish a methodology for measuring the health of corporate brands. Their multiple audiences and multidimensionality make them an altogether more complex issue. Complex, but important. My concluding section presents the argument for branding, in particular corporate branding, as an integral part of strategy.

CONCLUSION

It is fascinating to observe how the focus of management attention has changed during the past twenty years. The definition of what constitutes superior performance for commercial enterprises (growth and profitability) may remain relatively constant over time, but market dynamics ensure that the relative importance of the factors which produce that superior performance will change.

The declining returns to investments in total quality management (TQM) and business process re-engineering (BPR) are symptomatic of this. Techniques that used to deliver competitive advantage are now industry standard and do no more than establish the entry-level requirements for competing, particularly in manufacturing industries. In light of this, it is hardly surprising that each claim to have identified the algorithm for commercial success has always proven short-lived. Successive developments in management thinking have,

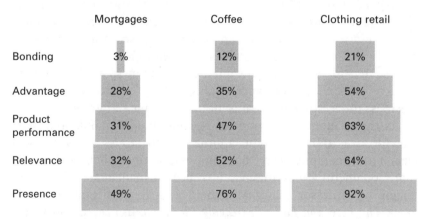

	Mortgages	Coffee	Clothing retail
Bonding	3%	12%	21%
Advantage	28%	35%	54%
Product performance	31%	47%	63%
Relevance	32%	52%	64%
Presence	49%	76%	92%

Figure 2.10 *Comparative brand strength across industries*

however, contributed to an improved understanding of the components necessary for commercial success. But 'necessary' does not mean 'sufficient' and while we are increasingly adept at explaining the causes of successful strategies with the benefit of hindsight, our abilities to devise successful strategies remain less developed.

What is clear is that the basis of competitive advantage has shifted rapidly over the past twenty years and introduced a whole new set of concepts to the management vocabulary: quality, time to market, lean production, benchmarking, supply chain management, customer satisfaction and loyalty, core competence and shareholder value. In retrospect, the 1980s was the 'decade of quality'. It began with the Western economies very behind the Asian markets in terms of the fundamental quality and consistency of manufactured output. The preoccupation with re-establishing the basis of US manufacturing competitiveness is best captured in the book *In Search of Excellence*, perhaps the first major business bestseller.

As quality standards rose and converged, the basis of business advantage shifted to organisations that were best able to employ their human capital and the underlying competences these people generated. The 1990s saw the publication of *The Fifth Discipline*, about learning organisations, and *The Core Competence of the Corporation*, about the underlying business capabilities that generate competitive advantage. The importance of a wider perspective on the drivers of business performance was encapsulated in *The Balanced Scorecard*, a seminal book from 1992. This recognised that purely financial measures are inadequate to explain superior corporate performance and it put forward a balanced scorecard process to identify and monitor the variables believed to have most influence. The scorecard proposed by Kaplan and Norton spans four dimensions: financial performance, knowledge of customers, internal business processes, and organisational learning and growth.

As the economic environment became more dynamic and more volatile, traditional analytic approaches to strategy – with their demand for comprehensive data and assumptions about a relatively static competitive environment – appeared inadequate. This is the theme of Professor Henry Mintzberg and, in particular, his 1994 book *The Rise and Fall of Strategic Planning*. In it he proposed the notion of 'emergent strategy' – strategy as something uncovered through experimentation rather than something designed and then implemented.

'The world is not an unsolved puzzle, waiting for the occasional genius to unlock its secrets. The world, or most of it, is an empty space waiting to be filled,' wrote Charles Handy in *Beyond Certainty* (1995). He echoes the importance of an organic approach to strategy and goes on to highlight the vital role played by the organisational culture in producing the kind of business environment that is suited to survival. In his 1997 article 'The Living Company', Arie de Geus gives one of the more persuasive articulations of the biological metaphor and how this perspective relates to business performance:

> Living, learning companies stand a better chance of surviving and evolving in a world they do not control. They make sense, especially because success now depends on mobilising as much of the intelligence at the company's disposal as possible. The high levels of tolerance inside the living organisation create the space for more innovation and learning. Creating that space is vital for brain-rich, asset-poor companies like law and accounting firms, credit card companies, and financial services companies, whose success depends on the quality of their internal communities. (*Harvard Business Review*, Mar/Apr 1997)

This conception of the organization as an organism has profound implications. In particular, the concept of command and control is no longer appropriate in an environment where communication occurs at all levels and in all directions. In her book *Biomimicry*, Janine Benyus puts it this way:

> What makes a mature community run is not one universal message being broadcast from above, but numerous, even redundant, messages coming from the grass roots, dispersed throughout the community structure. A rich feedback system allows changes in one component of the community to reverberate through the whole, allowing for adaptation when the environment changes. (p. 30)

The increasingly dynamic and volatile conditions in the market put a huge premium on organisations that are able to adapt. Figure 2.11 shows how the management of change has become the prime focus

	1960s	1970s	1980s	1990s
Focus	Operations	Resources	Competition	Change
Issue	Efficiency	Scarcity of capital	Performance	Renewal
Strategy	Processes and budgets	Planning	Execution	Innovation

Figure 2.11 *The evolution of CEO concerns*

of many CEOs. Branding has a vital role to play in the creation and nurturing of the type of internal, purposeful community that has the resilience to embrace change. By acting as ciphers of shared meaning, brands are able to create the sense of shared purpose that is needed if the human capital within an organisation is going to achieve its potential.

'The challenges of innovation and knowledge are profoundly human, social challenges. . . . Although management has always been at least as much an art as a science, time was when this reality could be ignored. That time is no more. The idea-led growth that now drives the global economy is not just about high-tech companies creating value through intellectual property. It is about managerial intelligence' (*Outlook*, June 1999; *Outlook* is published by Accenture, formerly Andersen Consulting). Brands are the art in the science of management – the means whereby our emotional needs as employees and customers can be met.

Summary of key points

- Brands are important because humans want to perceive meaning in what they do, and brands are powerful vehicles for communicating meaning.
  Brands decommoditise the underlying assets by augmenting them with a layer of emotional or symbolic meaning.
- Brands communicate on three principal levels: about what you will get; about what you will feel; about who your relationship is with.

- Branding is about the transformation of functional assets into relationship assets.
- A brand is the vehicle for the consumer's meaning, not the manufacturer's message.
- Product branding may be more visible, but service and corporate branding are more important.
- The decisive shift towards an information-based, brain-rich economy means that organisations depend on their ability to create vibrant, purposeful communities so as to unlock the human potential within the organisations.
- People are not 'assets' and are deeply resistant to attempts to manage them as if they were.
- Humans are social beings and work most productively when they perceive that they are part of a community of shared purpose.
- The corporate brand becomes the symbol of that common purpose and so supports the creation of an inspiring community.

BIBLIOGRAPHY

Aaker, David A., *Building Strong Brands* (Free Press, 1996)

Becker, Gary, *The Economic Approach to Human Behavior* (University of Chicago Press, 1978)

Becker, Gary, *The Economic Way of Looking at Behavior* (Hoover Institute Press, 1996)

Benyus, Janine, *Biomimcry* (William Morrow, 1997)

Buzan, Tony, *Make the Most of Your Mind* (Simon & Schuster, 1986)

Capra, Fritjof, *The Web of Life* (Doubleday, 1997)

Collins, James C. and Jerry I. Porras, *Built to Last* (Century, 1996)

D'Alessandro, David, *Brand Warfare* (McGraw-Hill, 2001)

De Geus, Arie, *The Living Company* (Harvard Business School Press, 1997)

Edvinsson, Leif and Michael Malone, *Intellectual Capital* (HarperBusiness, 1997)

Goleman, Daniel P., *Emotional Intelligence* (Bantam, 1997)

Hamel, Gary, *Leading the Revolution* (Harvard Business School Press, 2000)

Hamel, Gary and C. K. Prahalad, *Competing for the Future* (Harvard Business School Press, 1996)

Hammer, Michael and James Champy, *Re-engineering the Corporation* (HarperBusiness, 1994)

Handy, Charles, *Beyond Certainty* (Hutchinson, 1995)

Handy, Charles, *The Hungry Spirit* (Hutchinson, 1997)

Jones, Robert, *The Big Idea* (HarperCollins, 2000)

Kapferer, Jean-Noel, *Strategic Brand Management* (Kogan Page, 1998)

Kaplan, Robert S. and Norton, David P., *The Balanced Scorecard* (Harvard Business School Press, 1996)

Mintzberg, Henry, *The Rise and Fall of Strategic Planning* (Free Press, 1993)

Olins, Wally, *The New Guide to Corporate Identity* (Wolff Olins, 1995)

Ormerod, Paul, *Butterfly Economics* (Faber, 1998)

Pascal, Blaise, *Pensées* (Viking, 1995)

Peters, Tom, *In Search of Excellence* (Warner, 1988)

Peters, Tom, *The Circle of Innovation* (Vintage, 1999)

Rathwell, John M., *Marketing in the Services Sector* (Winthrop, 1974)

Ries, Al and Jack Trout, *Positioning: The Battle for Your Mind* (McGraw-Hill, 1986)

Roberts, Shirley, *Harness the Future* (John Wiley, 1998)

Rousseau, Jean-Jacques, *The Social Contract* (Penguin, 1987)

Rousseau, Jean-Jacques, *A Discourse on Inequality* (Viking, 1985)

Senge, Peter, *The Fifth Discipline* (Currency/Doubleday, 1994)

Womack, James P. *et al.*, *The Machine that Changed the World* (Rawson, 1990)

CHAPTER 3

Accounting for Intangible Assets

Lucinda Spicer and Caroline Woodward

INTRODUCTION

This chapter examines major developments in the measurement and recording of brands and other intangible assets in the UK over the years, current practices and how this area of accounting may evolve in the future. We also briefly consider the extent to which practice differs in various parts of the world. Whilst the UK was not the first country to account for intangible assets separately (this honour is due to the United States of America) it has seen a great deal of debate on this issue and, as such, has formed a good template for the rest of the world.

HISTORY AND DEVELOPMENT

Accounting for intangible assets in the UK is not a new concept although recent media debate may imply otherwise. The current issues attracting interest are the types of intangible assts featuring in business today and their relative importance in the context of a business's total assets.

The commercial accounting world has dealt with the most common intangible asset, goodwill, for many decades. A successful business, in any industry sector, is presumed to generate goodwill.

On a day-to-day basis this is reflected in its ability, inter alia, to retain customers, to acquire new ones, to generate profits and to increase its market share. The value of this 'internally generated' goodwill can only truly be measured when the business is sold. Prior to the accounting recognition of other intangible assets, goodwill was calculated and described as the excess of the purchase price paid for a business over the value of the net tangible assets acquired. At this stage it becomes 'purchased goodwill' and has typically either been written off immediately against the acquiring company's reserves or included on its balance sheet and subsequently amortised. Example 3.1 shows how goodwill arising is initially recorded.

Example 3.1

Company A has the following balance sheet:

Balance Sheet

Shareholders funds 500	Net tangible assets 500

It purchases Company B for 200 in cash. Company B has net tangible assets of 100; thus goodwill of 100 arises.

Company A's consolidated balance is thus:

Consolidated Balance Sheet

Shareholders funds 500	Net tangible assets	300
	(500–200 cash paid for B)	
	Net tangible assets	
	acquired	100
	Goodwill	100
		500

The Accounting Standards Board (ASB) now clearly distinguishes between 'internally generated' and 'purchased' intangible assets, of which more detail later.

Financial statements have also traditionally included other purchased intangible assets such as patents, copyright and software although often such items are included at cost rather than their value in use to the business. There has therefore been little or no debate over these items. In addition, research and development costs have normally been written off to the profit and loss account rather than being carried in the balance sheet.

The debate in the UK over whether or not brands and other intangible assets should be included in a company's balance sheet was at its most vigorous in the mid to late 1980s. This was a period of great activity in the area of mergers and acquisitions. The large, successful multinationals were expanding rapidly through acquisition, paying significant premiums over the balance sheet reported values of the net tangible assets acquired.

As noted above, in the UK at that time there were two principal ways to record the resulting 'goodwill' element of the purchase price in the acquiring company's accounts. The first was its immediate elimination against reserves, and the second was recording the amount in the balance sheet and amortising it over its expected useful life (usually a maximum 20 years). Neither of these options was particularly attractive to companies for the reasons discussed below.

The immediate elimination of the goodwill and other intangible assets element of an acquisition against reserves instantly reduces a company's net assets as shown in Example 3.2.

The balance sheet is thus apparently weakened whilst the company may well have been strengthened by the acquisition. Indeed, in 1988, *Ranks Hovis McDougall plc* pointed out that whilst its balance sheet showed net assets of £250 million, the stock market valued it at more than £1.5 billion. At the extreme, the advertising group *WPP* had negative net assets of £65 million at the end of its 1987 financial year after writing off goodwill arising on the purchase of *JWT Group*.

This accounting treatment, which was the preferred option under Statement of Standard Accounting Practice No. 22 at that time, caused increasing problems for acquisitive companies. Through simple arithmetic, as net assets reduced, gearing levels (the proportion of the company's debt finance to equity) increased. This led to companies

---

Example 3.2

Using Company A from the earlier example whose consolidated balance was as follows:

Consolidated Balance Sheet

Shareholders funds 500	Net tangible assets	400
	Goodwill	100
		500

If it now writes off the goodwill against reserves the consolidated balance sheet becomes:

Consolidated Balance Sheet

Shareholders funds 400	Net tangible assets	400

---

having difficulty in raising debt to finance acquisitions which in turn led to many acquisitions being either financed through equity issues or abandoned.

The alternative accounting treatment of capitalising the goodwill element of the purchase price was equally unpopular. Capitalised goodwill had to be written off to profits over its expected useful life; asserting that the useful life was indefinite was not permitted. Thus, under this method, companies' profits were reduced for a period of years through what many perceived as an artificial charge, notwithstanding the fact that the profit and loss account was probably showing clearly the benefits of the intangible assets acquired through enhanced sales and profits. As a final sting, the amortisation charge was not an allowable deduction in calculating profits chargeable to corporation tax and therefore gave higher effective tax rates than would otherwise have been the case.

The dissatisfaction felt within the corporate world at the limited options available to acquisitive companies manifested itself in a number of companies choosing to capitalise purchased intangible assets separately from goodwill. Example 3.3 below shows how this may be done.

Example 3.3

Using the previous example, if the assets acquired included brands valued at 50, the consolidated balance sheet would look like this:

Consolidated Balance Sheet

Shareholders funds 500	Net tangible assets	400
	Brands	50
	Goodwill	50
		500

Writing goodwill off to reserves, as before, the consolidated balance sheet becomes:

Consolidated Balance Sheet

Shareholders funds 450	Net tangible assets	400
	Brands	50
		450

Isolating the amounts related to these assets reduced the goodwill element of the purchase price and thus any write-off to reserves or charge to the profit and loss account. Better still, under the rules at that time, it was possible to claim that the brands and other intangible assets had an indefinite life and may well increase in value, thus obviating the need to amortise them. Indeed who would like to estimate the useful life of such brands as *Cadbury's* or *Coca-Cola*?

The first UK company to show acquired intangible assets separately on its balance sheet was *News International*, a subsidiary of News Corporation. In 1984, based on a valuation carried out by *Hambros Bank Limited* the company capitalised the titles, which it had acquired, including the *Sun* and the *Times*. At the time that *News International* acquired the *Times,* it had been making losses and had been out of print for some months but yet soon regained its former circulation levels thereby demonstrating that the masthead, or brand, had value distinct from the underlying business of newspaper publishing.

The next major company to follow was *Reckitt & Coleman plc* which, in 1985, included the values of acquired brands in its balance sheet.

Consumer brands leapt to the forefront of public debate in the summer of 1988 when *Nestlé* acquired *Rowntree* for more than twice its pre-bid capitalisation. At around the same time, *Grand Metropolitan plc* announced its intention to capitalise brands acquired since 1985, including *Smirnoff.* The company's stated intention was to attribute between 75% and 90% of the 'goodwill' element of the purchase price to the brands acquired and only to amortise the brands if the economic value showed a permanent decline over a period of 3 years. This policy was pursued by the directors under the true and fair concept to demonstrate fairly the effect of the acquisitions on the company's balance sheet.

Later in the same year, partly in response to an abortive takeover bid from *Goodman Fielder Wattie, Ranks Hovis McDougall plc* added a further dimension to the debate by becoming the first UK company to capitalise all its brands, both those acquired and those developed internally. This action generated heated debate within the accountancy profession and the business community. The accountancy profession in the UK was fundamentally divided on both how intangible assets should be valued and on whether they should be included in companies' balance sheets. Senior members of the profession called for urgent guidance from the *Accounting Standards Committee (ASC)*.

Whilst the branded products industry was generating discussion concerning the manner in which its brands were recorded and accounted for, other industries were choosing to capitalise their intangible assets, particularly the newspaper publishing industry. By the end of 1988 the titles, or mastheads, of almost all the main daily and Sunday newspapers in the UK had been valued and capitalised. The principal exceptions were the *Financial Times* and the *Guardian*.

Interestingly these valuations attracted little comment until the publication of the prospectus for *Mirror Group Newspapers (MGN)* in April 1991 prior to its flotation on the London Stock Exchange. The pro forma balance sheet of *MGN* showed net assets of £840.3 million (including flotation proceeds of around £250 million) of which the group's titles represented £625 million. Analysts at the time were sceptical and suggested that the valuation had been carried out merely to 'bolster' the balance sheet. However, at that time, several major publishing groups had publishing assets included in their balance sheets, which exceeded the net asset values shown in those balance sheets. Effectively, the value of publishing assets was hiding the fact that net tangible assets were negative. Details of three of these are shown in this table.

	Publishing assets (£bn)	Net assets (£bn)
News Corporation	5.2	4.4
Maxwell Communication	2.5	1.3
Reed International	1.5	1.4

Perhaps the most controversial approach adopted at the time, and that which caused the *ASC* the greatest concern, was the capitalisation of the trading names of businesses. This was first done by *Hodgson Holdings plc*, a quoted funeral director in their 1988 accounts. *Hodgson* argued that when buying a funeral business, goodwill and the value of the trade name are one and the same and valued the names of the 80 companies bought over the previous 8 years at £42 million. In the previous year's accounts, the cumulative effect of writing off the 'goodwill' on acquisitions has almost completely eliminated *Hodgson's* shareholders' funds. Conversely, the act of capitalising intangible assets previously written off results in a surge in a company's shareholders' funds. At the time, the other quoted funeral directors proposed to continue with their existing policies of writing off the goodwill on acquisitions against reserves. However, *WPP Group*, the marketing services and advertising company, which had acquired a number of companies with a significant reputation, was considering the approach adopted by *Hodgson Holdings*.

THE ACCOUNTING DEBATE

As noted earlier, during the 1980s the accounting for goodwill and other intangible assets in the UK was governed by Statement of Standard Accounting Practice (SSAP) 22, *Accounting for Goodwill*. The principal requirements of the standard are shown in the following extracts:

- No amount should be attributed to non-purchased goodwill in the balance sheet of companies or groups.
- The amount attributed to purchased goodwill should not include any value for separable intangibles. The amount of these, if material, should be included under the appropriate heading within intangible fixed assets in the balance sheet.
- Purchased goodwill should normally be eliminated from the accounts immediately on acquisition against reserves.
- Purchased goodwill may be eliminated from the accounts by amortisation through the profit and loss account . . . over its useful economic life.

The key point for acquirers of brands and other intangible assets is the ability to show them separately as fixed assets. If the intangible assets could be shown as fixed assets then, under the rules for accounting for fixed assets at that time, it was possible to assert that no diminution in value was likely and therefore that no depreciation or amortisation need be charged. So why then weren't all acquired brands and other intangible assets capitalised in the acquiring company's balance sheet?

Whilst we cannot say for certain what the reasoning was, an educated guess would suggest two main reasons – the concept of 'separability' and the lack of any widely accepted method of valuation.

The Second Schedule of the Companies Act 1989, which in the UK governs the format of company accounts, gave some clear guidance on what was meant by separable, or identifiable, assets as shown in the following extract:

- The identifiable assets and liabilities of the undertaking acquired shall be included in the consolidated balance sheet at their fair values as at the date of acquisition.

- In this paragraph the 'identifiable' assets or liabilities of the undertaking acquired means the assets or liabilities which are capable of being disposed of or discharged separately, without disposing of a business of the undertaking.

Thus if a brand or other intangible asset could be sold without selling the underlying business, it could be capitalised on the company's balance sheet. This seems fairly straightforward and there is ample market evidence to show that consumer brands may be sold separately from the underlying business. However, to be fair, it was less common at that time than it is now for pure brands to be sold without selling also the underlying production facilities and associated business. Whilst this did not mean that a brand could not be sold separately, it did continue to nurture the doubts concerning separability. Furthermore of course there was the question of how to quantify the goodwill element of the purchase price attributable to the brand, which brings us back to valuation.

The valuation of intangible assets for balance sheet purposes was controversial at that time, not least because it was a new concept and there was little or no guidance as to how they should be valued. Indeed those companies that included brands and other intangible assets in their balance sheets disclosed very little about how the values had been arrived at.

Ranks Hovis McDougall disclosed most fully their approach, which was developed with the help of Interbrand, a specialist consultancy. Their method involved taking the average earnings from a brand over the previous 3 years and multiplying it by a factor that reflected the branded product's market position and the amount of advertising support. A product with a longer life expectancy in the market would attract a higher multiple than one which was 'here today, gone tomorrow'. Ranks Hovis McDougall said that the value was based on current figures and took no account of the brand's future earning capacity and thus was not a 'market value'. Indeed the company stated that the market value of their brands was 'considerably more' than the figure included in the balance sheet.

Ranks Hovis McDougall's fairly full and frank disclosure provided much ammunition for criticism for both those against brand valuation and those for it. The opponents of brand valuation suggested that if the value was not a market value then it was really of no use to anyone. The methodology was criticised by many as being 'too subjective' for balance sheet purposes. Mr William J. Kornitzer of specialist valuers American Appraisal (UK) expressed a mixed reaction in a letter to the *Financial Times*. He explained that it was common practice in the USA to place acquired brands and other intangible assets on the balance sheet. He expressed surprise that British companies should be the first to place internally developed brands on the balance sheet, a practice not permitted in the USA, but welcomed the concept as a step towards helping shareholders to better understand a company's worth. He said, however, that what was 'more surprising' was the choice of methodology; he noted that 'accepted methodologies' had been devised for valuing brands and suggested that the application of these would be preferable. So, even within the valuation profession there was no consensus on valuation methodology.

In December 1988 the ASC disclosed that it planned to issue guidelines aimed at bringing uniformity to the way in which companies accounted for brands and other intangible assets. The chairman of the ASC, Mr Michael Renshall, expressed the committee's concern about the separability of brands and other intangible assets when he made the following comment regarding the recent trend towards capitalising brands in the balance sheet: 'The ASC looks at this with some anxiety. . . . It's very difficult to separate brand names from the intrinsic goodwill, the essence of a business. We hope that companies will consider very carefully before they revalue intangibles.'

Whilst detailed guidelines were some way off in December 1988, the ASC promised provisional guidance in January 1989.

On 26 January 1989 the ASC published a news release setting out its provisional views on accounting for brands and other intangible assets. This preliminary guidance did not have the force of an accounting standard but effectively put pressure on companies to conform. The ASC asked companies to desist from making brand valuations until further work had been done into how values are calculated. The committee called on companies to include information about intangible assets in the notes to the accounts rather than in the balance sheet.

These proposals included a requirement for companies to depreciate assets such as brands unless they could persuade their auditors that the assets would retain their value indefinitely. A further proposal was to require companies to be consistent in their valuations, i.e. not to include some assets at a valuation and some at cost. There had been considerable public comment that companies valued only the assets that they chose thus creating a confusing or misleading balance sheet. The committee did state their belief that companies should include in their balance sheets brands and other separable intangible assets acquired in a takeover, as a value could be placed on them with some certainty since it could be calculated from the purchase price.

The proposals met with strong disapproval from the corporate world. The principal point of dissent was the need to depreciate or amortise the value of brands and other intangible assets through the profit and loss account. Comments made by the finance directors of leading companies included:

- It's very much accountants dictating what we should do.
- Brands are more likely to increase in value than to decrease.
- We are committed to our brands and put considerable resources into sustaining them; we don't believe that there is any need to write them down.
- Costs of brand support are already expensed through the profit and loss account; there is no need to write down the asset as well.

Crucially, on the very same day that the ASC issued its news release, the London Stock Exchange issued a statement designed to encourage companies to include intangible assets in their balance sheets. The Stock Exchange's listings agreement, the Yellow Book, requires companies to seek shareholder approval for acquisitions and disposals exceeding certain size limits. One of these is when the assets involved exceed 25% of the company's own. In its statement of 26 January 1989 the Stock Exchange announced that companies could add in intangible assets when calculating asset size. Previously such inclusion had only been at the discretion of the exchange's quotations committee.

In February 1989 the Institute of Chartered Accountants commissioned a research project from the London Business School entitled 'Accounting for brands – clarifying the basis of valuation'. This was followed a year later by a technical release from the ASC which was to form the substance of two exposure drafts. The content of the documents was well leaked in advance and reaction to it was so severe that, controversially, the ASC amended the content before final publication.

The ASC proposed initially that brands should not be recognised on the balance sheet. Their reasoning for this was that the whole area of valuing brands was 'inherently extremely subjective'. The technical release stated:

> Brands may be of considerable value to the business but that does not in itself imply that they should be accounted for as discrete assets. In practice it is seldom meaningful to value such assets individually because their particular value is to be found only when they are used in conjunction with all the other assets and attributes which comprise the business.

The ASC recommended that an intangible asset should only be recognised on the balance sheet as a fixed asset in its own right if it could be discretely recognised, if its characteristics were clearly distinguishable from those of goodwill and other assets and if its cost could be measured independently of goodwill, of other assets and of the earnings and cash flows of the relevant business or business segment. Any intangible assets, which met the requirements and were thus capitalised, still had to be amortised over a period not exceeding 20 years along with goodwill.

The business community reacted so badly to the leaked proposals that, the following day, the ASC agreed to amend its proposals to say that all acquired brands may be capitalised. However, they must still be written off over a maximum of 20 years. Mr Michael Renshall, ASC chairman, said 'We are listening and recognise the issues raised by industry. Realism dictates that we do not try to persuade people that brands should not be shown on the balance sheet. Such information can be helpful for shareholders.'

In May 1990 the ASC issued Exposure Draft (ED) 47, 'Accounting for goodwill' and ED 52, 'Accounting for intangible assets'. The latter, had it been adopted as a standard, would have severely limited a company's ability to include intangible assets on its balance sheet. Under ED 52 intangible assets could only be recognised in the annual accounts if their historical cost was readily ascertainable; their characteristics were clearly distinguishable from other assets; and their cost could be measured independently of goodwill, of other assets and of the earnings of the relevant business or business segment. These conditions, the ASC admitted at the time, would exclude many intangible assets, including brands.

Reaction to ED 47 and ED 52 was severe: 93% of corporate respondents opposed ED 47 and 80% of corporate respondents opposed ED 52. Those opposing the proposals argued primarily that, where large sums were spent on maintaining and developing the value of an acquired business, a requirement to amortise a significant amount of the investment over an arbitrary period of time had no economic meaning. The view was expressed by many that goodwill and other intangible assets should only be written off if there was evidence that their value had declined.

Whilst ED 47 and ED 52 were out for comment, the ASC was replaced by the Accounting Standards Board (ASB). This body took on the task of developing financial reporting standards to cover a number of issues, including those of goodwill and other intangible assets, although it took some while for the ASB to pick up the gauntlet.

In the meantime industry added its own contribution to the debate in the form of a study prepared by Arthur Andersen. This study, entitled 'The Valuation of Intangible Assets', was published in January 1992. It was sponsored by 11 top companies: Cadbury Schweppes, Grand Metropolitan, Guinness, Pearson, Ranks Hovis McDougall, Reckitt & Coleman, Reed International, SmithKline Beecham, Thorn EMI, United Biscuits and United Newspapers each of whom clearly had a vested interest in being able to capitalise brands and other intangible assets. The stated purpose of the report was clear:

To increase public confidence in the capability of valuers to identify and value separable intangible assets. If this initiative is effective, standard setters will view more positively than hitherto such developments in generally accepted accounting and reporting practices.

The report concluded: 'Many intangible assets are identifiable, separable and capable of systematic valuation.'

In the report Andersens were trying to increase awareness in the business and regulatory community of the methods adopted by valuers in preparing intangible asset valuations and to produce a set of guidelines that could form the basis of guidance notes for professional valuers. The guidelines explained the principles and methodologies involved in valuing intangible assets whilst the report emphasised the importance of objectivity, the need for a standard approach, cost-effectiveness, consistency, reliability, relevance and practicality. The report accepted that 'valuation of all assets is subjective, especially . . . intangible assets where there is often no open market. Given the subjectivities involved in such circumstances, adequate guidelines and standards are required.'

Almost 2 years later, in December 1993, the ASB issued a discussion paper entitled 'Goodwill and Intangible Assets'. In this paper the ASB took a strong stance and, notwithstanding all the comment and research which had gone before, stated that in the board's opinion 'certain intangible assets such as brands and publishing titles could not be disposed of separately from a business and, further, that there was no generally accepted method of valuing such intangible assets.' The latter comment was in direct contradiction to the statement made some 5 years earlier by Mr William Kornitzer of American Appraisal (UK) (referred to earlier) which informed the readers of the *Financial Times* that there were accepted methodologies for valuing intangible assets. Clearly the ASB was not yet convinced on this point. The discussion paper therefore proposed that intangible assets acquired as part of the acquisition of a business should be subsumed within the value attributed to goodwill.

The discussion paper took a more lenient view on goodwill, which as noted above was now to include other intangible assets. The board proposed 6 possible methods of accounting for goodwill:

1. Capitalisation and amortisation over a finite period.
2. Capitalisation and annual impairment reviews.

3. A combination of methods 1 and 2 with method 2 only being used in the special circumstances where goodwill has an indefinite life believed to exceed 20 years (*sic*).
4. Immediate elimination against reserves.
5. Immediate elimination to a separate goodwill write-off reserve.
6. Transfer to a separate goodwill write-off reserve, with annual reviews of recoverability and any impairments being charged to the profit and loss account.

Unsurprisingly the proposals for brands and other intangible assets met with strong opposition. Once again corporate respondents stressed the importance of such assets to their business and the need to account for them separately. There was no consensus from the response to the proposals for goodwill although the majority favoured methods that involved some form of capitalisation rather than immediate write-off.

The ASB took account of the views expressed by those who had responded to the discussion paper. In consultation with preparers, users and auditors of financial statements the board developed its proposals. The chosen method for accounting for goodwill was method 3 – capitalisation with a combination of amortisation for goodwill with a finite life and annual impairment reviews for goodwill with a life expected to exceed 20 years. In regard to other intangible assets, the board accepted the argument for separate accounting. It therefore proposed that intangible assets could be recognised separately from goodwill if they met the legal and conceptual separability requirements and could be measured reliably. However, in order to prevent abuse, the board proposed that these assets should be accounted for in the same way as goodwill.

These revised proposals were field tested by seven large acquisitive groups following which they were further refined. The refined proposals were set out in a working paper entitled 'Goodwill and Intangible Assets' issued in June 1995 for public debate. There was broad support for these revised proposals and they formed the basis of Financial Reporting Exposure Draft (FRED) 12, which was issued in 1996.

The majority of respondents to FRED 12 were broadly in support of the approach. There were still some who favoured immediate elimination of purchased goodwill against reserves and some who wished to capitalise internally generated brands and other intangible assets. However, the principal change made before FRED 12 became a standard was to remove the procedures relating to impairment reviews to a separate standard requiring impairment reviews of all fixed assets, both tangible and intangible.

Thus, in December 1997, FRS 10 'Goodwill and Intangible Assets' was published, followed by FRS 11 'Impairment of Fixed Assets and Goodwill' in July 1998. Both standards were effective for accounting periods ending on or after 23 December 1998.

CURRENT ACCOUNTING AND REPORTING REQUIREMENTS

FRS 10 applies to goodwill and all other intangible assets except oil and gas exploration and development costs, research and development costs and any other intangible assets specifically covered by other accounting standards. FRS 10 deals with the following issues in respect of intangible assets:

- Recognition rules
    - Intangible assets developed internally
    - Intangible assets purchased separately
    - Intangible assets acquired as part of the acquisition of a business
- Valuation rules
- Amortisation and impairment rules
- Financial statement disclosures

FRS 10 defines intangible assets as

> non-financial fixed assets that do not have physical substance but are identifiable and are controlled by the entity through custody or legal rights.

The definition is important firstly to distinguish intangible assets from tangible assets and secondly to distinguish intangible assets from goodwill. This is important because different accounting rules apply to each category and the rules for capitalising and revaluing intangible fixed assets are more difficult to comply with than those for tangible fixed assets.

As noted earlier, separability is a key criterion for the identification of an intangible asset. FRS 10 states:

An identifiable asset is defined by companies legislation as one that can be disposed of separately without disposing of a business of the entity. If an asset can be disposed of only as part of the revenue earning activity to which it contributes, it is regarded as indistinguishable from the goodwill relating to that activity and is accounted for as such.

The final sentence is hardly helpful but then the ASB never made any secret of the fact that they did not believe that brands and other intangible assets were distinct from goodwill. In general, the issue of separability is less critical than it was pre FRS 10 in that internally generated intangible assets may not be capitalised and all acquired ones must be (whether as goodwill or as other intangible assets). This means that *Diageo* can capitalise the drinks brands which it has acquired but may not capitalise the *Guinness* brand as it was developed internally. However, there are differences in the accounting treatment in that non-amortisation of intangible assets is permitted, subject to an annual review for impairment, whilst the non-amortisation of goodwill contravenes the Companies Act and accordingly requires a 'true and fair over-ride'. This means that the company's directors and auditors must agree that a truer and fairer view of the company's results for the year and financial position is shown by not complying with the law than would be shown had the law been complied with.

Certain brands and other intangible assets are clearly more separable than others. The food and drinks industries regularly buy and sell brands without disposing of a business and here brands might be considered some of the most 'separable' intangible assets. However, having regard to the extract from FRS 10 above, it is difficult to see how their disposal would not have at least a temporary impact on the revenues of the underlying business. Nevertheless FRS 10 refers to brands as examples of intangible assets that are unique and therefore likely to be regarded as identifiable assets in certain circumstances. A multi-brand business can clearly sell individual brands without selling the underlying business but what of the single-brand business? Well that business could sell its brand and continue in business as before but dealing in unbranded goods, for example as an 'own brand' manufacturer in the food industry; profits will probably be lower but the business is still there. Where the brand name is the same as the company name it is more difficult in certain circumstances to see how the brand may be separated from the rest of the business. For instance *Sainsbury's* is a well-known brand but it is difficult to see how that brand could be disposed of without the underlying business. The brand could certainly be exploited through licensing or franchising but those activities are not disposals. In contrast *SmithKline Beecham* could sell the *Beecham* trademark without selling the underlying business.

Another key issue is that the intangible asset must be under the control of the business through custody or legal rights. In respect of items such as trademarks, patents, licences, and so on, control is secured by legal rights that restrict the access of others. The standard specifically excludes such assets as a company's workforce as, although undoubtedly valuable to the business, it is not under the control of the business.

Before dealing with the rules of FRS 10 applicable to most intangible assets, we shall deal briefly with the exceptions. FRS 10 defines one group of intangible assets, which need not follow the rules of FRS 10 but instead are capitalised and depreciated in the same manner as tangible fixed assets. The standard calls these 'assets that have a readily ascertainable market value'. FRS 10 defines a readily ascertainable market value as one which derives from:

- An asset belonging to a homogeneous population of assets that are equivalent in all respects; and
- An active market in those assets, evidenced by frequent trans-actions.

Examples of such assets might include milk quotas, taxi licences and airport landing rights.

In practice, most intangible assets are unique to the business which controls them and therefore do not meet the requirement of being part of a homogeneous population. Furthermore, although the volume of transactions in intangible assets is increasing, most intangible assets do not have a readily ascertainable market value. Thus, these provisions of FRS 10 are applicable to only a small minority of intangible assets.

Apart from the exceptions discussed above, FRS 10 identifies three classes of intangible asset. We review the rules for each of these below.

Internally developed intangible assets

Under FRS 10 an internally developed intangible asset may only be capitalised if it has a readily ascertainable market value, as defined above. In all other cases, the costs of developing the asset must be written off to the profit and loss account as incurred. As mentioned earlier, in practice few intangible assets have a readily identifiable market value. The capitalisation rules for internally developed assets mean that the costs of obtaining patents, licences, and so on, may not be capitalised.

Purchased intangible assets

FRS 10 states that an intangible asset purchased separately from a business should be capitalised at its cost.

Assets acquired with a business

The standard states that an intangible asset acquired as part of the acquisition of a business should be capitalised separately from goodwill if its value can be measured reliably on initial recognition.

The normal principles for estimating the fair value of identifiable assets in acquisition accounting set out in FRS 7 apply to both tangible and intangible fixed assets. FRS 7 states that where an intangible asset is recognised, its fair value should be based on its replacement cost, which is normally market value. FRS 10 requires the application of a third criterion, reliable measurement, over and above the separability and control issues discussed earlier.

The standard further distinguishes between those assets that have a readily identifiable market value (the minority) and those that are unique (most acquired intangible assets). The former should be included at their market value on the date of acquisition whilst the latter are limited to an amount which does not create or increase any negative goodwill, i.e. the acquisition price represents a ceiling for the values of all assets acquired. This means that an acquisition made at a bargain price, or the fact that the intangible assets acquired may be worth more in the hands of the new owner, may not be reflected in the values ascribed to the different assets acquired.

Value measurement

We referred earlier to the distinct scepticism expressed by the ASB about the reliability of valuations of intangible assets where, in their opinion, there is no readily ascertainable market value. This flavour is still evident in FRS 10. In addition to the ceiling placed on the valuation as noted above, there is still a need to consider whether the value may be measured 'reliably'. FRS 10 does accept that certain entities, who regularly buy and sell unique intangible fixed assets, will have developed their own reliable techniques for valuing them that would allow them to be capitalised separately from goodwill on an acquisition. Other entities, which are not in a position to demonstrate that they have developed valuation techniques from such regular activity, may include the value of acquired intangible assets within the value attributed to goodwill. The onus is on companies to demonstrate that they can measure the value of their intangible assets reliably.

The standard refers briefly to valuation techniques which may be used to measure the value of intangible assets. It mentions techniques based on 'indicators of value' such as multiples of turnover or the present value of royalties that might be received from licensing out the asset. FRS 10 requires the method or methods adopted to be disclosed in the financial statements. Methods of valuation are discussed in more detail later.

Revaluation of intangible assets

With the exception of the minority of assets with a readily ascertainable market value no revaluation of intangible assets is permitted after their initial recognition at cost or fair value on acquisition. Assets with a readily ascertainable market value may be revalued to their market value when that changes from the figure shown in the balance sheet. If this procedure is followed it must be carried out regularly and consistently, i.e. on an annual basis and recognising decreases as well as increases in market value!

The majority of purchased intangible assets will therefore not be revalued upwards. Even where the new management relaunches or revitalises a tired brand, the increase in value may not be recognised in the balance sheet. Furthermore, the costs of such a relaunch or redevelopment must also be written off as incurred and may not be capitalised.

Amortisation

The object of FRS 10 is to ensure that capitalised intangible assts are written off to the profit and loss account over the period that their value is depleted. This principle applies to both intangible assets purchased separately and those purchased as part of the acquisition of a business. Intangible assets are required to be written off systematically over their useful economic life. The useful economic life of an intangible asset is presumed, by FRS 10, not to exceed 20 years. However, this presumption is rebuttable and a longer life, or even an indefinite life, may be used where the asset can be demonstrated to be more durable.

The useful economic life of an intangible asset is defined in FRS 10 as 'the period over which the entity expects to derive economic benefits from that asset.' Whilst FRS 10 contains the presumption that an intangible asset's economic life will not exceed 20 years this is not intended to be a default option. The inherent uncertainties in estimating the useful economic life of an intangible asset are recognised by the standard and a shorter period should be used, if relevant, although the standard also discourages the use of the uncertainties involved as an excuse to write assets off over an unrealistically short period.

Intangible assets that are amortised over a period of 20 years or less should be reviewed for impairment at the end of the first full financial year following their acquisition. In subsequent years an impairment review is only required if adverse events indicate that the carrying value may be overstated and thus that a write-down may be appropriate.

An economic life in excess of 20 years, or even an indefinite life, may be chosen only if the following two conditions are met:

- The durability of the intangible asset for the longer, or indefinite, period can be demonstrated; and
- The intangible asset is capable of continued measurement.

Clearly the assumptions underlying the projections of future performance become more vulnerable the longer the projected period is. In certain branded industries the rate of development is so fast that consumer demand cannot be reliably predicted over a long period of time whilst others have demonstrated their staying power over the years. FRS 10 gives examples of factors which contribute to the durability of a brand or other intangible asset. These factors refer to the nature of the business, the stability of the industry, the effect of future competition, the typical lifespans of the products involved and the extent to which business acquisitions overcome any market entry barriers.

The above factors often combine to give an overall impression of the durability of an intangible asset. Selection of an economic life of more than 20 years will usually require a business, industry and products with a long track record of stability and achievement and reasonable barriers to entry. In addition there is a need for commitment to invest as necessary over the expected useful life of the asset such that it retains or enhances its market position. Long lives can be seen to be relevant for brands such as *Cadbury's, Schweppes, Persil* and *Gordon's* and also for publishing titles such as the *Times* and the *Daily Telegraph.* However, in the case of relatively new brands or publishing titles launched into highly competitive and volatile marketplaces where customers often have a short attention span a shorter life is probably both appropriate and prudent.

An intangible asset which is depreciated over a period of more than 20 years, or not depreciated at all, must undergo an annual impairment review to ensure that the asset is still worth at least the amount at which it is carried in the balance sheet. If the value has been impaired then the asset must be written down in the balance sheet to its recoverable amount. The write-down is charged to the profit and loss account.

As well as justifying the durability of the brand or other intangible asset, in order to claim an economic life of more than 20 years, the second condition must be met. This requires that the asset must be capable of continued measurement so that the annual impairment reviews may be carried out. These reviews must be feasible and implemented. Thus, if the directors are of the opinion that the cost of carrying out the impairment reviews outweighs the benefit they should not elect for an economic life in excess of 20 years.

Obviously, in addition to considering the above factors in determining an asset's economic life the period for which the asset is legally available must be taken into account. For some intangible assets the rights remain in force indefinitely or can be continually renewed, for example trademarks relating to brand names. Other assets have finite periods for which the current owner has exclusivity in the marketplace, for example drug patents which can rarely be renewed and once they expire, competitors can immediately launch their products. In today's pharmaceutical world the length of a patent has become almost irrelevant as competing similar products are in the market within months of the original being launched. Periods of exclusivity have reduced from years to a matter of months. This clearly has implications both for the economic life attributed to a drug patent and, more crucially, its ability to generate the expected earnings for the owning business.

FRS 10 states that where legal rights are in force for a finite period, the economic life of the intangible asset may not be longer unless 'the legal rights are renewable and renewal is assured'. In all other cases the economic life of the asset must be the length of time for which the legal rights are in force. The standard limits the circumstances in which the renewal of a legal right can be regarded as assured to those where:

- The value of the intangible asset does not reduce as the expiry date approaches.
- There is evidence that the legal rights will be renewed.
- There is no evidence that any conditions that have to be complied with for renewal have been or will be breached.

The standard states that the method of amortising an intangible asset should reflect the expected pattern of its depletion. However, the straight-line method should be chosen unless another method can be shown to be more appropriate.

Impairment reviews

As noted above, FRS 10 requires all intangible assets to be reviewed for impairment. The procedures for these reviews are set out in a separate standard, FRS 11 'Impairment of Fixed Assets and Good-will'. The procedures for intangible assets are closely linked to those for goodwill. The requirements differ depending on whether the asset is being amortised over a period greater or lesser than 20 years. If an asset is either not amortised or amortised over a very long period, there is a greater risk of impairment than if the asset is written off over a shorter period. This is why the requirements for impairment reviews are more onerous for assets amortised over a period exceeding 20 years. We look below at the different requirements.

Assets amortised over less than 20 years

Intangible assets must be reviewed for impairment at the end of the first full financial year following their acquisition. The timing of this review coincides with that required under FRS 7 on the acquisition of a business when the fair value exercise on all the assets and liabilities of the acquired business should be completed. Such a review is also required if the intangible asset has been acquired on its own.

The first year review has two stages. The first stage requires management to formally consider whether the acquisition has met expectations. This is done by comparing actual performance with the forecasts or projections made at the time of the acquisition. In addition consideration is required as to whether any unexpected adverse events or changes in circumstances have occurred which cast doubt on the recoverable amount of the capitalised intangible asset. If the acquisition passes this test there is no need to proceed to the second stage.

In subsequent years management must consider whether events or changes in circumstances indicate that the amortised carrying amount of the intangible asset may not be recoverable. If there is no such indication then no further work is required. If there is such indication then a full impairment review is required. Details of this are provided below.

FRS 11 gives a list of examples of situations that may indicate that the asset has become impaired. Naturally this list is not exhaustive and management needs to consider any significant changes to the business or to the environment within which it operates. The main indicators suggested are:

- Operating losses or net cash outflows incurred or expected
- Adverse change in the business or market, for example the entrance of a new competitor
- Adverse change in any indicator of value used to measure the fair value of an intangible asset on acquisition
- Adverse change in the statutory or regulatory environment
- Commitment to a significant reorganisation
- Major loss of key employees
- Significant increase in market interest rates or rates of return

In the case of brands impairment may be indicated by any one of a number of factors, which might include:

- A fall in the volume of sales or market share
- A fall in the profit margin obtainable on sales
- The launch by a competitor of a generic alternative to the branded product
- The launch by a competitor of a competing branded product
- The withdrawal from the market of the product due to safety or similar concerns
- The need for increased marketing and promotion costs to support existing levels of sales and margins

If any factors are identified which indicate that the carrying value of the asset may have been impaired, a full impairment review must be carried out. If, following such a review, impairment is confirmed then the carrying value of the asset must be written down its recoverable amount.

Assets amortised over more than 20 years

Intangible assets which are amortised over a period exceeding 20 years, or which are not amortised at all, must be subjected to a detailed annual impairment review. Full details of the procedures required for a full impairment review are set out in FRS 11 but are summarised briefly below. An impairment review is a check on the recoverable amount on individual assets or groups of assets and includes capitalised intangible assets, goodwill and tangible assets. It follows the usual principle that the balance sheet carrying value of an asset should not exceed its recoverable amount. The recoverable amount is measured by reference to the expected cash flows which the asset is expected to generate through use (value in use) or through disposal (net realisable value) whichever is the higher. If an asset's balance sheet carrying amount exceeds its recoverable amount then it is impaired and should be written down to the higher of its value in use or its net realisable value.

The net realisable value of an asset (the amount for which it could be sold, net of the costs of realisation) may be difficult to determine in the absence of an established market for the asset from which a reliable value might be determined. Remember that FRS 10 does not consider it possible to establish the market value of unique intangible assets such as brands and publishing titles. Where a net realisable value cannot be determined directly, FRS 11 requires that the recoverable amount of the intangible asset be calculated solely by reference to its value in use.

Where both a value in use and a net realisable value can be calculated it is important to calculate both. This is because the carrying amount of the asset in the balance sheet needs only to be compared with the higher of the two values mentioned above. Thus even if the market value of the asset is lower than its value in use, the asset only needs to be written down to the extent that the value in use is lower than the balance sheet carrying amount.

Measuring the value in use of some intangible assets is not straightforward, as certain assets do not generate cash flows in isolation. If intangible assets cannot be reviewed for impairment individually, they should be reviewed in groups of similar assets that generate income streams that are largely independent of each other. These are referred to by the standard as income-generating units.

The principal steps in a full impairment review are as follows:

1. Identifying separate income-generating units.
2. Establishing balance sheets for each income-generating unit, comprising the net tangible and intangible assets plus the allocated portion of purchased goodwill.

3. Projecting the future cash flows of the income-generating unit and discounting them to their present value.
4. Comparing the present value of the cash flows calculated above with the net assets of the income-generating unit and recognising any shortfall as an impairment loss.
5. Allocating any impairment loss to write down the assets of the income-generating unit in the following order:
   - Purchased goodwill
   - Capitalised intangible assets
   - Tangible assets

If an intangible asset, which is required to have a full annual review for impairment, is not actually expected to be impaired then the procedures may be simplified in the second and subsequent years. After the first full review has been carried out, subsequent reviews may be performed by updating the calculations used for the first review. Indeed FRS 10 notes that, if there have been no adverse changes since the first review, it may be possible immediately to determine that no impairment has occurred.

Recovery of past losses

It may be that during the life of an intangible asset the original assumptions concerning its economic life may be considered to have been too prudent or that an impairment, originally thought to have been permanent, now appears to have been only temporary. FRS 10 envisages both such situations and details how they may be dealt with.

If an intangible asset appears to have been amortised too quickly, its economic life may be extended. However, the remaining carrying value must be amortised over the revised period only. FRS 10 does not permit previous amortisation charges to be credited to the profit and loss account.

In limited circumstances impairment losses in respect of intangible assets may be credited to the profit and loss account. The exception to the general rule is again with those few assets that are deemed to have a readily ascertainable market value. Such assets which may have been impaired are allowed to be written back up to the extent that their net realisable value, calculated by reference to their market value, subsequently increases to above their carrying value in the balance sheet.

For all other intangible assets (including goodwill) the limited circumstances where their impairment losses may be reversed are where (a) an external event caused the original impairment loss and (b) subsequent external events clearly and demonstrably reverse the effect of that event in a way that was not foreseen at the time of the original impairment calculations. An example of this would be when a brand was written off because the product had been withdrawn following a health scare that raised concerns about its safety. At the time management believed that the withdrawal was permanent and therefore that the impairment was also permanent. The safety concerns subsequently prove to be unfounded, the brand is reintroduced to the market and regains its market position. In these circumstances the brand may be recapitalised and the credit taken to the profit and loss account but only to the level at which the brand was recorded prior to the impairment loss.

FRS 10 requires the reason for any reversal of impairment loss to be disclosed in the financial statements together with the assumptions upon which the recoverable amount shown in the accounts is based.

Financial statement disclosures

FRS 10 requires the following disclosures in respect of intangible assets in the financial statements:

- The method of valuation
- For each class of intangible asset:
  - The cost or revalued amount at the beginning and at the end of the period
  - The cumulative provisions for amortisation or impairment at the beginning and at the end of the period
  - A reconciliation of the movements showing additions, disposals, revaluations, transfers, amortisation, impairment losses and reversals of past impairment losses
  - The net carrying amount at the balance sheet date

- The methods and periods of amortisation and the reasons for choosing those periods
- The reason for, and effect of, changing useful economic lives
- The reason for, and effect of, changing amortisation methods
- Where an intangible asset is amortised over a period exceeding 20 years, or is not amortised, the reasons for rebutting the 20 year presumption
- Where a class of intangible assets has been revalued, that is only those with a readily ascertainable market value, the following details are required:
  - The year in which the assets were valued, the values and the bases of valuation
  - The original cost or fair value of the assets and the amount of any provision for amortisation that would have been recognised if the assets had been valued at their original cost or fair value
  - The name and qualifications of the person who valued any intangible asset that has been revalued during the year

SUMMARY OF UK ACCOUNTING REQUIREMENTS

The table on the next page summarises the detailed requirements given above.

Current UK practice

So, given all the emotion regarding the capitalisation of brands and other intangible assets in the 1980s, what is the current position now that the UK has accounting standards to deal with the issue? Well, perhaps unsurprisingly, there has been little change. The original mavericks who capitalised their acquired brands before the existence of FRS 10 continue to do so. Indeed those companies will easily fall into the category of being able to demonstrate that they have developed suitable methods to establish a reliable measurement of acquired brands. Of course, the capitalisation of internally generated brands is not permitted. Those companies which had previously capitalised their internally generated brands had to write them off as a prior period adjustment upon the introduction of FRS 10.

	Intangible assets with a readily ascertainable market value	Unique (or most) intangible assets
Initial recognition at cost or fair value		
Internally generated	Yes	No
Purchased separately	Yes	No
Business acquisition	Yes	Yes, but only if it can be measured reliably and does not create or increase negative goodwill
Subsequent revaluation	Yes, to market value	No
Impairment loss allocation	Not written down below net realisable value	Written down fully before any tangible assets
Impairment loss reversal	Yes, if net realisable value increases above impaired carrying value	Yes, but only if an external event is reversed in a way that was not originally foreseen

There have been few other companies who have been prepared to separate out the value of acquired brands and other intangible assets from the goodwill element of the purchase price of an acquisition. Most have simply capitalised the goodwill arising and are amortising it over a period of 20 years.

Why has so little changed? Well, in the face of an accounting standard that grudgingly permits the capitalisation of acquired intangible assets under certain limited circumstances there is little encouragement to do anything other than accept the capitalisation of the goodwill element of a purchase price and be done with it. Given that FRS 10 still expresses concerns over the separability of brands many companies are taking a cautious stance and electing not to capitalise them. These companies' auditors appear quite happy to support such a decision. Indeed, under FRS 10, a company which chooses to call the entire premium over the net tangible asset value paid on an acquisition goodwill is far less likely to attract comment on or a qualification to its accounts than one which chooses to separate out and capitalise the value of brands and other intangible assets acquired. In addition to the doubt cast by FRS 10 over the separability of brands and other intangible assets, there is also scepticism expressed over whether such items may be reliably measured. Furthermore, this scepticism is directed at management. If management are not *themselves* capable of reliably measuring the value of their acquired intangible assets then it is deemed inappropriate for the value of those assets to be included in the accounts. This is perhaps rather unfair; management are not expected to be expert in the valuation of their tangible assets, they are permitted to use an expert valuer and to rely on such expert's opinion. There are experts in the valuation of intangible assets so why may management not rely on them?

Another disincentive is the current UK taxation system, which does not distinguish between goodwill and other acquired intangible assets. Under the current rules neither the amortisation of goodwill nor the amortisation of acquired intangible assets is a permitted deduction in arriving at the profits chargeable to corporation tax. This is not a new situation; the tax system has always disallowed such charges to the profit and loss account. However, pre FRS 10 companies were able to capitalise brands and other intangible assets, whether acquired or internally generated, and to claim that no amortisation was required, as the assets were not expected to decline in value. Remember also, in those days, any goodwill arising on an acquisition was usually written off directly to reserves and such goodwill was usually relatively small once the value of other intangible assets had been separately capitalised. Thus no amortisation was charged in the accounts in respect of these items resulting in the profits chargeable to corporation tax being closer to those shown in the financial statements than they would otherwise have been.

There is, however, potentially some good news on this front. Details of this are set out below in the discussion on proposed new tax legislation.

Thus, in the UK at the present time companies report details of their intangible assets in a variety of different ways. Some companies are showing separately the value of acquired intangible assets and some do not. The assets that are shown will be amortised over a variety of different periods and some will not be amortised at all. All acquisitive companies will be incurring a high effective tax rate (the corporation tax charge expressed as a percentage of the profit before tax shown in the profit and loss account) unless they are one of the few claiming that no amortisation charges are required for their acquired intangible assets. Finally of course, those companies which have acquired brands and other intangible assets will be showing apparently stronger balance sheets than those will which have developed strong brands internally.

UK taxation issues

In June 2000 the Inland Revenue published a technical note entitled *Reform of the taxation of intellectual property, goodwill and other intangible assets.* That document considered in broad terms how earlier ideas on reforming the tax treatment of intellectual property could be extended to a wider range of intangible assets including goodwill. Over 80 responses were received to that note, including those from the Institute of Directors, the Confederation of British Industry, the Chartered Institute of Taxation, the tax faculty of the Institute of Chartered Accountants in England and Wales and the major accounting firms. The responses were generally positive and so the Inland Revenue produced a second technical note, dated 8 November 2000, entitled *Reform of the taxation of intellectual property, goodwill and intangible assets: the next stage,* details of which were announced in the Chancellor's pre-budget speech in November 2000. The second note considered firmer options for taking the reform forward in the light of the responses received to the earlier note. Further comments were invited on this note by 20 December 2000; again, most business and professional organisations responded positively. The government has recently published draft clauses for further consultation. Unfortunately, these proposals appear to have dropped the earlier intention to make the reliefs available on share purchases and restrict them to asset purchases only. This will make the changes to the legislation applicable to only a minority of acquisitive corporate taxpayers. It will be interesting to see how the business community reacts to this and whether pressure will be brought to bear on the government to reinstate its earlier plans for the reliefs to be available on share purchases.

The background to the proposed reforms is clear. Britain's companies are increasingly founded on assets such as brands, which are valuable but intangible. The rising importance of intangible assets reflects the shift from manufacturing companies to a service-based economy. Companies are moving from dependence on large holdings of physical assets such as factories and machines towards greater reliance on such assets as knowledge. A recent survey of leading companies by Middlesex University Business School found that goodwill, brands and other intangible assets accounted for £56 billion of assets in companies' balance sheets in 1999 compared with £23 billion five years previously.

This shift in emphasis in the business world has created some anomalies in the tax legislation. Whilst companies can gain tax relief on expenditure on plant and machinery there is no similar relief for the purchase of intangible assets. The government says that a main aim of the reforms is to redress the balance. It proposes to model its approach on the accounting standards thus permitting similar treatment for intangible assets, provided that they are acquired as part of a business acquisition, as that allowed for tangible assets acquired.

The stated aim of the reform is to align the system of taxation of intangible assets with the accountancy treatment as far as possible in order to simplify the system and to provide relief for a wider range of business expenses. Most respondents to the note of June 2000 were in favour of the reforms encompassing all the assets covered by FRS 10 although there was some doubt expressed about whether or not goodwill should be allowed relief. Intangible assets were formally defined for Inland Revenue purposes in the Finance Act 2000 as

> any asset which falls to be treated as an intangible asset in accordance with normal accounting practice. For this purpose, normal accounting practice means normal accounting practice in relation to the accounts of companies incorporated in any part of the United Kingdom.

The June 2000 technical note made it clear that the government could see significant simplification and modernisation gains in following the accounting treatment for intangible assets. The majority of the respondents to the note agreed with this approach and wanted to see as few departures from this principle as possible. In addition, the government wants to rely on the figures in the financial statements as far as possible as, the greater the departures therefrom, the less an accounts-based system delivers the simplification and compliance cost benefits that the government seeks.

In broad terms the Revenue wants to build on the legislation used in the new provisions on mobile phone licences and telecommunications capacity rights in the last Finance Act. The basic provision of Schedule 23 to the Finance Act 2000 states that:

> Amounts that may in accordance with normal accounting practice be taken into account in determining profit or loss for accounting purposes in respect of
>
> (a) expenditure on the acquisition of a right to which this section applies, or
> (b) receipts from the disposal of any such right,
>
> shall be treated as items of a revenue nature for tax purposes provided that they are so taken into account in any relevant statutory accounts of the taxpayer.

This means that amortisation charges for goodwill (if permitted) and other intangible assets will be allowed as a deduction in computing the profits of a company chargeable to corporation tax. This is a major step forward and will be a welcome relief for acquisitive companies which have seen their profits dramatically reduce following the introduction of FRS 10. *Vodafone*, the telecommunications group, saw profits reduced in 1999 by £2.3 billion in respect of goodwill write-downs.

An interesting development is that the Inland Revenue wants to take their proposals beyond those assets encompassed by FRS 10. This could provide an opportunity for substantial savings by high-technology companies. The government has let it be known that it sees the provision of tax reliefs in the area of intangible assets as a tool to assist in the development of such businesses.

The current proposals extend the scope of the new rules beyond the range of fixed assets covered by FRS 10 in three areas:

1. The government wants to follow the accounts in allowing relief for expenditure on internally generated intangible assets as it is written off to the profit and loss account. Under current legisltion, the Inland Revenue would in some cases regard the expenditure as giving rise to an asset or advantage of an enduring nature and thereby as capital, even though it did not give rise to an asset under the provisions of FRS 10. This would include a range of costs, including internal software development, where the accounting standard does not permit capitalisation. A possible approach suggested by the Inland Revenue is to allow expenditure incurred in creating an intangible asset as it is charged to the profit and loss account, if that asset is one that, if purchased by another company, would fall to be classified as an asset under FRS 10. Whilst this may be of immediate appeal to high-technology businesses, as is the government's wish, it may also apply to those companies who are developing brands internally.
2. The government wants to include the incidental costs of acquiring intangible assets within the new rules. The costs of acquiring specific assets will generally be capitalised as part of the total asset cost and so relief can readily follow the accounts treatment. More difficult issues arise with regard to the incidental costs of acquiring a business, where these costs will generally be subsumed into the goodwill figure and be difficult to separately identify.
3. Where a transaction is aborted, the incidental costs will generally be written off to the profit and loss account and, under current Inland Revenue rules, would be disallowed as capital. The government intends that such costs should qualify for relief insofar as they relate to goodwill and other intangible assets.

Whilst the new proposals address comprehensively the theoretical approach to aligning the accounting and taxation systems for brands and other intangible assets, the Inland Revenue has also thought carefully about the practical implications. The current technical note addresses the issues of fairness to both purchaser and vendor, potential abuse of the proposed system and those companies which have existing intangible assets being amortised under FRS 10. Their suggestions for each of these cases are outlined below.

Fairness to both purchaser and vendor

The Inland Revenue recognises that the application of the accounting rules in a given transaction may result in different values being recognised by the vendor to those recognised by the purchaser. This is because the purchaser is required to comply with FRS 7 and allocate fair values to the assets and liabilities acquired.

The Revenue's stated objective is to achieve symmetry on the two sides of any transaction. In other words, to ensure that the expenditure on intangible assets on which the purchaser is obtaining relief broadly matches the amount being taxed as a receipt in the hands of the vendor. In particular, the Revenue is concerned to prevent value shifting between assets in order to gain a tax advantage.

Abuse of the proposals

During discussions on the new proposals it has been suggested that the introduction of tax advantages might lead to companies driving down their estimates of intangible assets' useful economic lives in order to obtain a tax advantage. Whilst this has been dismissed by respondents as a misplaced concern, particularly with regard to UK quoted companies, the Revenue feel that certain safeguards are necessary to prevent abuse.

The government recognises that one of the advantages in following the accounting rules is that this gives flexibility in matching amortisation rates to the wide range of intangible assets, which may fall within the proposed regime. This will mean, in general, that the Revenue will follow the amortisation rates adopted by businesses where these follow correct accounting practice. However, the government also recognises that this flexibility may result in aggressive write-offs and indeed to an additional burden for companies in answering questions from the Revenue on their assets and related accounting policies.

The Revenue recognises the possibility that the availability of tax relief may provide an incentive for companies to take an unduly pessimistic view of the economic life of an intangible asset, or to choose a more aggressive method of amortisation than the recommended straight-line method. Whilst recognising that the market itself will provide some discipline for quoted companies, the Revenue propose some checks in the new system to counter any abuse. The only real option proposed at the moment is to set a floor of say 5 years on write-off rates. This is not an option that the Revenue favours as it is crude and removes to an extent the advantage of flexibility. Respondents to the technical note are invited to comment on the need for such a measure and the best method of implement-ation, if appropriate.

Transitional rules for existing assets

The government's aim is for the transition to the new system to be swift, fair and simple. However, these are potentially conflicting demands and the rules for existing owners of intangible fixed assets need to be addressed.

Most respondents to the June technical paper wanted the new reliefs to be available immediately to existing owners of intangible assets but many were concerned that an immediate switch would lead to significant tax becoming payable on a disposal of these existing assets. The loss of capital asset status for these assets was thought likely to deter companies from disposing of them in the short term.

The Revenue has therefore proposed alternative treatments for such assets and has invited comment on which of them is preferable.

The first proposal is that existing assets are brought in to the new regime immediately at their current book value. Subsequent amort-isation will be allowable for tax purposes in accordance with the new rules. On a disposal of any asset after the new regime has started the profit chargeable to tax will be the amount shown in the accounts. That is the net proceeds of disposal less the book value shown in the accounts. In the case of an asset which was already being amortised prior to the commencement of the new system, an additional de-duction would be available equal to the amount of amortisation charged before the new system commenced.

The alternative proposal considers continuing the existing capital gains system for existing assets in a modified form. Gains attribut-able to the period before the introduction of the new system would be charged as capital gains whilst those arising after the introduction of the new system would be considered to be income and taxed as such. This approach may be less attractive to companies if for no other reason than that the 'market value' of the asset at the date of introduction of the new system would have to be calculated in order to apportion the gain between the two periods.

The new proposals appear to be a welcome development for many businesses today and will hopefully result in positive changes in the way that businesses account for their brands and other intangible assets.

Comparison with accounting requirements in other jurisdictions

Outside the UK the two largest accounting standard setting bodies are the Financial Accounting Standards Board in the USA and the International Accounting Standards Board. The Financial Accounting Standards Board had a standard relating to the treatment of intangible assets in a company's financial statements long before the advent of FRS 10. The International Accounting Standards Board issued an exposure draft covering the treatment of intangible assets, ED 60, in June 1997 six months before FRS 10 was published in the UK. International Accounting Standard 38 was issued in July 1998, effective for accounting periods beginning on or after 1 July 1999.

Whilst the various standards are not in complete harmony, there are happily more similarities than differences amongst them. In the following paragraphs we briefly compare and contrast US and international generally accepted accounting procedures for brands and other intangible assets with the requirements of FRS 10 and 11.

US requirements
The current US requirements are set out in APB 17 and FAS 121. As under FRS 10, capitalisation and amortisation of purchased intangible assets is required provided that they meet the definition of an asset, can be clearly identified and are capable of reliable measurement.

- An intangible asset acquired separately is required to be included in the financial statements at cost.
- If intangible assets are acquired as part of a business acquisition then those assets must be included in the financial statements at their fair value.
- The US rules do not permit the capitalisation of internally generated intangible assets.

- US rules do not permit the revaluation of intangible assets even if there is an active market.
- The maximum economic life permitted for an asset is 40 years.
- Impairment reviews are required whenever changes in events or circumstances indicate that the carrying amount of an intangible asset may not be recoverable.

The Financial Accounting Standards Board has published a new Exposure Draft on Business Combinations and Intangible Assets which brings the requirements for amortisation of intangible assets closer to those under FRS 10. It proposes a rebuttable presumption that intangible assets have a useful life not exceeding 20 years and would permit an indefinite useful life in certain restricted circumstances. The proposed rules for impairment reviews of intangible assets are those which apply to tangible assets and are broadly similar to those under FRS 11.

International requirements

As many companies outside the US use International Accounting Standards (IAS), particularly when reporting outside their domestic jurisdictions, and the European Union is proposing to make it compulsory for EU companies to prepare their accounts using IAS, it is appropriate here to consider how IAS compare to UK standards.

International Accounting Standard 38 requires that an intangible asset should be recognised if, and only if, it is probable that future economic benefits attributable to the asset will flow to the enterprise and the cost of the asset can be measured reliably. This requirement applies to all intangible assets, whether acquired externally or developed internally. IAS 38 includes additional recognition criteria for internally generated intangible assets. This standard also deals with research and development costs, which are the subject of a separate standard in the UK.

- IAS 38 specifies that internally generated goodwill, brands, mastheads, publishing titles, customer lists and similar items should not be recognised as assets.
- Intangible assets acquired separately are required to be included in the financial statements at cost.

- An intangible asset acquired as part of an acquisition may be included at its cost or fair value if that amount can be measured with sufficient reliability for separate recognition.
- If an active market exists for the intangible asset in question then the current market price will determine the value for inclusion in the financial statements.
- If no active market exists then the fair value of the intangible asset may be estimated by reference to recent transactions in similar assets.
- An intangible asset may only be revalued where there is an active market in that type of intangible asset.
- Amortisation of intangible assets is mandatory; it is not possible to assume an indefinite life for the asset.
- The period of amortisation should represent the best estimate of the intangible asset's useful life, with a rebuttable presumption that it will not exceed 20 years.
- In rare cases, where the 20 year presumption is rebutted, the enterprise should disclose its justification and review the carrying amount for impairment on an annual basis.
- Impairment reviews are to be carried out in accordance with the provisions of IAS 36. This standard requires that the recoverable amount of any asset should be estimated whenever there is an indication that the asset may be impaired. An impairment loss should be recognised whenever the carrying amount of an asset exceeds its recoverable amount.

Thus it can be seen that the major accounting standard setters do not differ widely in their rules applied to brands and other intangible assets. Each revision of each standard brings the three closer together which is of course desirable in today's business environment as businesses rarely operate, or even list their shares, solely in their national market.

VALUATION OF INTANGIBLE ASSETS

As noted earlier, one of the concerns expressed by the ASB is that there are no reliable methods of valuing brands and other intangible assets. This chapter would be incomplete without some reference to the valuation methods employed to value intangible assets.

FRS 10 refers briefly to valuation techniques that may be used to estimate fair values of intangible assets at the date of acquisition. It mentions techniques based on 'indicators of value' such as multiples of turnover or the present value of royalties that would be payable to licence the asset from a third party. Whilst the latter is a commonly used method of valuation, the former is more of a means of expressing or cross-checking a valuation arrived at by first principles.

It is worth noting at this point that most commonly used valuation methodologies calculate the economic value of an asset to its current owner rather than a market value. Whilst in some cases economic value and market value will be similar, in many cases they will not be.

There are several methods commonly used by specialist valuers to value intangible assets. Typically a valuer will use as many as possible in any particular valuation to ensure the robustness of the final conclusion and for each to act as a cross-check against the others. The most commonly used methods are:

- Replacement cost
- Cost saving approach
- Relief from royalties
- Premium profits
- Capitalisation of earnings
- Market transaction comparison

Whilst most intangible assets lend themselves to the use of one or other of the above approaches brands, as a class of assets, can be valued by most of these methods. Each of the methods is described briefly below.

Replacement cost

Under this method, an asset which has been built internally, and for which cost records are available, may be valued by reference to the cost of building it today. Whilst this does not allow the asset to be capitalised in the company's official financial statements (as it is an internally generated asset) it can be a useful measure for management decision making. Examples of assets which lend themselves to this approach are engineering drawings, patents and copyrights.

Cost saving approach

This approach has some similarities with the premium profit approach described below but focuses principally on the costs saved by virtue of using the asset in the business. The calculated cost savings are projected forward and then discounted back to the present day. Alternatively, the cost savings may be multiplied by a factor if projections are not available. Assets which lend themselves to this approach include business systems and proprietary technology.

Relief from royalties

Under this method, the asset is valued by reference to the amount which could be obtained by licensing out the right to exploit the asset to a third party or, alternatively, by reference to the royalties that the owner of the asset is relieved from paying by virtue of being the owner rather than the licensee. A notional royalty rate is set at a percentage of revenues, which is then applied to the projected revenues for the intangible asset. The estimated royalty stream is then discounted to a present-day value to arrive at a market value.

The method is relatively simple especially if the asset is already subject to licensing arrangements. If there is no prior history of licensing the valuer researches available information concerning licensing of similar assets to obtain a royalty rate. In practice this can be difficult as such information is rarely publicly disclosed and it is often not possible to tell which party is bearing the promotional expenditure. Another way of approaching this method in the absence of a known royalty rate, is to select a rate which gives an acceptable rate of return to each party as this is clearly the basis of any commercial arrangement.

Whilst the approach noted above can be looked at from either the position of the licensor or the licensee it is important to distinguish between those parties for valuation purposes. The royalty rate and the discount rate applied to the cash flows will depend on whether the value to the licensor, or owner, or licensee is being calculated. It is also important to consider which party will be bearing the costs of supporting the intangible asset, e.g. marketing.

In general an owner or a licensor has additional rights over the asset thus implying additional value through enhanced cash flows. However, the valuer should keep in mind the extent of any royalty agreements when valuing on behalf of the licensee; worldwide rights to an asset are tantamount to ownership.

In general terms a licensor has 'pushed away' some of the risk as he is now only risking the fact that the licensee will not pay the expected royalty stream due to sales or cost fluctuations. Therefore the discount rate applied to the royalty stream may be estimated as lower than that for the owner who is entitled to the entire 'super profit' earned by the brand.

Assets which lend themselves to this valuation approach are brands, patents and computer software.

Premium profits

The premium profits approach determines the value of the intangible asset by capitalising the additional profits generated by the business owning the brand or other intangible asset over and above those generated by similar businesses which do not have the benefit of a branded product. There are various ways in which the premium profits may be calculated: by reference to a margin differential, identifying the premium price charged in comparison to that charged for generic and other non-branded products, and comparing the return on capital employed earned by the branded business to that earned by the non-branded business.

In determining the additional profit attributable to the intangible asset it is important to ensure that the comparable companies selected are reporting their results under similar accounting standards so as to avoid potential distortions. Often it is also helpful to consider different measures of profit such as gross profit less intangible asset support, earnings before interest, tax and depreciation, and so on, depending on the industry and to give additional data for comparison.

The calculated premium profits are then discounted to the present day, or multiplied by a factor if projections are not available, to arrive at a value for the intangible asset in question.

It is important that the premium profits identified are specifically attributable to the brand or other intangible asset and not to some other factor such as an efficient production facility or distribution network that relates to the business as a whole.

The best comparable companies for this approach are those involved in 'generic' or non-branded products. These are increasingly difficult to find as 'own-label' products such as those produced for *Marks & Spencer, Sainsbury's,* and so on, are considered to be brands in their own right. Where 'generic' producing companies do not exist then further adjustments need to be made in calculating the values. For example, the valuer may take account of premium pricing – a tin of *Heinz* baked beans retails at more than a tin of *Sainsbury's* baked beans.

Intangible assets which lend themselves to this methodology include brands, patents and copyrights.

Capitalisation of earnings

The capitalised earnings method involves estimating the maintainable earnings that accrue to the intangible asset. A capitalisation factor is then applied to those earnings. This factor should take account of all the factors listed below which will determine the future earning capacity of the intangible asset and the risks involved in achieving those earnings. Intangible assets which lend themselves to this methodology are brands, customer lists and software licences. In determining the value of a brand under any method various factors need to be taken into account; here are some of them:

- The market sector
  Brands that are established in a sector which generates high sales, margins or both will clearly have a higher value than those in markets that are restricted in terms of total sales volume or profit margins. Expanding markets for a product will enhance the prospects for exploiting the brand name and will therefore increase its value.

- Durability

  If a brand name has lasted for many years it is likely to have considerable customer loyalty and will therefore support a higher valuation than a name which may be currently fashionable but that is in a sector where fashions change rapidly and brand names are less durable.

- International spread

  A brand name that is also known in markets other than its domestic one has a larger potential customer base than one which is purely a domestic brand and thus is likely to be more highly valued.

- Market position

  The brand leader in any market segment is likely to be the most valuable brand in that segment. Indeed it is often said that, in most consumer markets, only the top two or three brands really have any value.

- Advertising support

  The amount of advertising support needed by the brand to support its market position is a key factor in determining its value. If a brand is not supported then it is likely to lose value. However, a declining brand can require ever increasing advertising support to maintain its position to a point where it is no longer economic to do so.

- Changes in external factors

  Many brands are vulnerable to changes in legislation or environmental factors. However, if a brand has demonstrated its resilience to such factors in the past it may well do so again in the future.

- Competition

  The introduction of alternatives to the branded product or indications that competitors are increasing spending on rival products may well affect the value of the brand.

- Flexibility

  The flexibility of the brand or the degree to which it can be extended to other products is also a key indicator of success and therefore value.

Market transaction comparison

This approach considers actual market transactions in similar intangible assets. A multiple of turnover or profits associated with an intangible asset is derived from actual transactions and then applied to the asset being valued. Many intangible assets are indeed unique and so this method may not be suitable for all valuations. Furthermore, pure transactions in intangible assets are infrequent and often only scant details are publicly disclosed. However, where relevant information exists, this method can produce a useful cross-check to values arrived at using other methods.

CHAPTER 4

Internet Branding: Brave New World?

Shonaig Macpherson

WHAT IS MEANT BY AN INTERNET BRAND?

The phenomenal growth of the internet has led to nothing short of a revolution in the commercial world. The most recent research shows the value of internet transactions doubling every year until 2004, up to £1,000 billion pounds per annum (Forrester Research). The new economy will have a material impact on traditional brands, the strategies used to develop them, and the way they are protected and enforced.

Across a wide range of areas, the internet has run a coach and horses through traditional legal rules. At its simplest, the reason for this happening is that the internet pays no heed to national boundaries while laws are by their nature territorial. This leads to an almost infinite number of potential conflicts; for example, a website set up in the UK may be entirely legal in this country, but illegal in the country where it is accessed. Take a simple example. Boots, the high-street chemist, has '3 for 2' offers on items such as toothpaste. But these offers are illegal in Germany, and Boots is likely to be breaching German law if a consumer in Germany can access its website and take up such an offer.

While it is hoped that recent proposals put forward by the European Commission may do away with future problems of this kind within the European Union, the problem will inevitably keep arising in relation to the rest of the world, at least until appropriate international treaties are signed. Another real example of this jurisdictional problem came in a recent case in the US. In many parts of the US, gambling is illegal. Thus, when setting up an online casino in Antigua, the proprietors were careful to expressly state that customers should not use the site in states or countries where gaming is illegal. This warning, however, was not sufficient to prevent the New York Supreme Court from finding that the website proprietors were committing an offence.

The internet is global, so it stands to reason that unless laws are identical in every country, the legality or the illegality of website content will always be a subject for consideration. At this time, and pending further legislative moves, the uneasy truth is that the only viable policy is to try to manage the risks involved. In essence this involves distinguishing theoretical risks from actual risks, assessing the extent of the actual risks and taking action in respect of those actual risks while ignoring the rest.

Before considering how the internet has impacted upon branding and business models, it is perhaps worth briefly considering what is meant by a 'brand' in modern parlance. In its traditional sense, a brand was taken to be interchangeable with a trademark, meaning that a brand was a mark put onto a product to distinguish that product from other, otherwise similar, products. This is no longer taken to be the case, whether in traditional or internet businesses. A brand is now taken to encompass not only a physical trademark, but all the other significant features which, when taken together, distinguish a company and its products from those of its competitors.

Perhaps this is best illustrated by the example of IBM, which became synonymous with the mantra: No one ever got sacked for buying IBM. The emphasis here is startling. There is no claim that IBM produce superior products, or that they have cutting-edge technology. Rather, the claim implicit in this statement is simply that IBM is a solid, credible company with products which have a track record of working. When the term 'brand' is used, it is this wider concept which is imagined.

The advent of the internet was heralded by many as the death knell for brands. Owners of brands have in the past expended significant effort and money on building sophisticated distribution channels to protect their brand's integrity, in reality ensuring that prices remained artificially high. Retailers were often required to invest in specially designed outlets, advertising and other activities to support brand development. The internet has been seen as a means to dilute these practices as, arguably, substantially less capital is required to develop global reach for a business. The domain name and website are a window on the world and they are relatively easy for anyone to access.

The reduced capital requirement to establish and maintain a business over the web allows savings to be passed on to customers as reduced prices. It also cuts out the middleman – the effect of dis-intermediation. The internet allows the consumer to make price comparisons quickly and efficiently before committing to purchase. It was thought that the internet would return us to a discounter's paradise of price-driven offers as purchaser power exerted itself. This was an easy conclusion but somewhat misplaced. The internet is not a user-friendly environment: it can be difficult to navigate around. A brand that remains in the mind after a transaction is more likely to secure repeat visitors. For many consumers the internet is an unknown. A consumer is more likely to gravitate towards a brand he already recognises and trusts.

Successful internet businesses are expending as much as any other business on traditional routes of promotion to establish a brand. A brand connotes images of quality, integrity and value, all just as relevant on the internet, for after the initial flurry, consumers will seek the same qualities as in the terrestrial world. They will return to a website that they trust, a website offering integrity and value. This makes it extremely important to treat brand protection as seriously on the web as in the terrestrial world.

The conflict between trademarks and domain names

The conflict between national laws and the global internet leads to particular problems in relation to branding. The major problem is that there is a definite tension between national trademark regimes and the domain name registration system. Trademark registrations are effectively based on distinctiveness and proof of ownership, and they have always been seen as an entitlement to use a particular brand (in the old sense). In contrast, domain names were originally long strings of numbers, like telephone numbers. Because people found it difficult to follow this, words were then used. With the discovery that the internet could have commercial uses, domain names became the basis of the new internet brands.

This raised many new issues, as the internet was initially unregulated. Consequently, domain names are still largely administered on a first come first served basis, subject to the recent requirement that the applicant has a bona fide right to use the name (see p. 151). Only one person can own the .com domain name in respect of any particular brand, no matter where they are in the world and no matter what use they make of it.

In contrast, numerous businesses may use the same trademark in the UK, due to the fact that the UK Trade Marks Register is divided into 42 different classes of goods and services, and a mark can be granted in each separate class. Take the trademark 'Paragon'. At the last count, there were 51 registered trademarks on the UK Trade Marks Register which consisted solely of the word Paragon, whether in word or stylised form. These marks are owned by a number of separate companies. Each of these companies is entitled to monopoly rights in Paragon in the UK in relation to the kinds of goods or services for which they have a registration.

When you consider that each country has its own trademarks system, and not every user of the mark will have registered it (though they may have unregistered rights in the name), it seems clear there are literally hundreds of businesses using the Paragon brand. In this case the lucky owner of the domain name is an American company involved in the internet itself. Naturally, proprietors of Paragon trademarks in the UK (not to mention any users of Paragon in other countries) are unlikely to be happy with this. Not only can they not use their trademark as a .com domain name, but their national trademarks are quite possibly being infringed by the American companies' use of the domain name paragon.com (see p. 145).

Another interesting feature of internet branding is the move from distinctive names to generic names. It is a feature of trademark law around the world that if the trademark is descriptive of the goods or services being offered, or is laudatory, it should not be granted. For example, it would not be possible to register the word 'business' as a trademark. Unless, of course, the trademark 'business' is not used in relation to business per se, i.e. it is not used in a descriptive sense. For example, it ought to be possible, in principle, to apply for a trademark for the word 'business' in relation to clothes, or food and drink. But beware of the argument being raised against you that such use is deceptive. However, it is possible to acquire the domain name 'business.com', and to use it in the sure knowledge that no one will have prior trademark rights in it, provided they use the mark in a descriptive sense. These generic terms have been sold for vast sums; for example, the domain name business.com was recently sold for a record $7.5 million.

Another major advantage with using descriptive names in internet brands is that they are somewhat intuitive. If an internet user wanted to find out news, they might try the web address www.news.co.uk. This will in fact take them to the *Times* newspaper site, but the basic desire – to find out the news – has been met. By acquiring the intuitive domain name, the *Times* can swell the numbers of visitors to its site. Obviously the use of these generic domain names is not so attractive to companies that already have well-developed brand names in the terrestrial world, and who will rely principally on these brands to generate traffic to their sites; these companies will wish to continue protecting them. However, for new businesses these generic addresses offer the prospect of attracting and keeping customers on the basis that 'it does exactly what it says on the tin', and gives them effective monopoly rights, at least in relation to the internet, because every domain name is unique. Also, the domain name is immediately recognisable because of its descriptiveness, seldom true of a very new business.

What type of domain name should you choose?

A major question in relation to branding is the choice of suffix. For example, would the name generic.com be better than generic.co.uk? All generalisations are dangerous, including this one, but it's probably fair to say that the .com suffix is perceived as being far superior to the others. It smacks of credibility, particularly when used next to a single word. The domain name generic.com says, 'I am established, I have been into the internet from the beginning, and I am a serious player.' The range of suffixes is continually expanding to cope with demand. Recent major developments include the launch of the generic.ws domain, and this will shortly be followed by the generic. eu domain. Some commentators have argued that this will dilute the value of .com domain names, but I believe the exact opposite: the proliferation of variations will make .com even more desirable, and even more of a necessity for global players. The generic.ws domain (with ws purporting to stand for 'world site') is in fact an attempt to compete with the primacy of the .com sites, using the suffix originally assigned to Western Samoa, in the same way that the suffix .uk was allocated to the United Kingdom.

The decision of which domain name to adopt is becoming more and more expensive by the day. Quality one-word domain names, such as generic.com, now regularly command fees from $10,000 up to $1 million. Indeed, a number of domain names have cost more than a million dollars.

In certain limited circumstances, however, the name generic.co.uk may be acceptable, or indeed preferable, especially if you intend your website to do business in the UK only. For example, a number of UK banks prefer to use [name].co.uk domains to emphasise that they are only authorised to carry on banking business in the UK. By using a domain name of this kind, they at least put users in other countries on notice that they are located in the UK, which may be enough to prevent customers illegally opening an account. generic.org and generic.net domains can also be useful, especially when they are used in relation to industry organisations and the internet.

ESTABLISHING AND MAINTAINING AN INTERNET BRAND

Choosing your brand

For most internet companies, securing the perfect domain name is crucial. This will generally become synonymous with the business, and it will uniquely identify the company in the minds of its customers, be they other companies or consumers. It will be the essence of the brand. Registering a domain name is simple and cheap, and there are many websites where you can register it. Domain names can be purchased immediately on line using a credit card. It usually costs well below £50 per domain name (even cheaper if that service provider is going to host your website). The registration lasts for two years and then needs to be renewed.

Securing a domain name may be a difficult task, given the number of domain names already registered. But the key point is that, once secured, a domain name is not in itself a green light to use the site. This is the case even if you also own a company name which is very similar. For example, a company called Paragon Tiles Limited will not automatically have the right to trade as paragon.co.uk. Trademark and other rights should always be investigated.

Many businesses have found, to their cost, that buying and using a domain name without first checking the trademark position can cost them very heavily indeed. They have invested in a brand based around a domain name only to find there are prior trademark or other rights in that name which belong to another company. In this situation the only options are to rebrand or to enter into some kind of arrangement with the trademark rights owner, whether this is a licence to use the mark, or an assignment of the mark in its entirety. Trademarks give monopoly rights to their owner in a given field, and provided they are valid, they cannot be avoided without the consent of the owner.

Establishing your brand

The dawn of the internet has led to radical new business models being introduced. Traditional models based on organic growth, expanding premises, low costs and high margins have been cast aside in favour of launching global strategies with high-profile advertising campaigns from day one. Investors have, up till recently, been willing to accept the high risks involved because of the promise of great riches to follow.

One important part of this is the international and cross-border nature of the internet, which promises worldwide renown in return for lower upfront costs. In the real world, businesses can be constrained by geography. Businesses would start up in a locality; those that provided competitive goods and services flourished, and those that couldn't died. Profit would be made and reinvested, monies could be borrowed from banks, and the business could expand. Many of today's global giants started this way. Only in very unusual markets could people talk of global markets.

Now, thanks to the internet, and more specifically the World Wide Web, a website can be accessed from anywhere in the world the minute it goes live. If you want to buy a black pudding, you now have alternatives to the local butcher: among others, Jack Scaife & Son of Yorkshire will accept and meet your internet order. The monopoly of the local butcher is challenged, competition is introduced, and prices can only come down. There is also the opportunity for a small Yorkshire butcher to establish a renowned brand among black pudding connoisseurs throughout the world.

There are interesting parallels between how a local business builds a brand and how an online business builds a brand. Take a record shop. In the real world, turnover for a business is generated through a number of different factors, such as how many people go past the shop, how many people have the shop recommended to them, and how the shop is advertised. Advertising will generally be in specialist magazines, along with local initiatives such as poster adverts and leaflet drops. Whether or not people come back to the shop will then be determined by whether they like what they find there. In the virtual world, the object remains the same: businesses want to catch passing traffic, and they want to ensure that existing customers return. What is different is the way this business is generated and kept. At the risk of stating the obvious, no one is likely to find your online record shop if you don't draw it to their attention. This can be done in several different ways.

Payments to a search engine

Payments can be made to web search engines to ensure that your website is included on their listing. Perhaps you've arranged with Yahoo! that when a particular word, say 'news', is typed into the search engine, then a range of sites will be produced which include that word or phrase. It can be difficult for small start-up websites to be included by major search engines, and many search engine providers now carry out reviews of the websites. The sheer volume of web content means that even once a site is listed by a search engine, an individual search may come back with so many options that your site will go unvisited.

Meta-tags in your website

You can insert meta-tags into your website. Meta-tags are hidden pieces of code which internet search engines look for when compiling information about websites. An online record store might try to attract surfers using the meta-tags 'record shop', 'CD' and 'music'. Meta-tags have been the subject of considerable speculation because some internet businesses put the trademarks of competitors into their sites. For example, an online bookshop might use the meta-tag 'amazon' or 'amazon.com', so when a surfer searches for 'amazon' the unrelated bookshop will be shown as a hit. It is possible that using the trademark of another in this way will amount to a trademark infringement, depending on the law of the country or countries where the trademark is registered, so considerable care should be taken before embedding the trademarks of other companies into the code for your site.

A multitude of adverts

You can advertise your website in many different ways, using new or conventional media. For example, it is common for sites to host banner ads, which effect links between sites, often known as hyperlinks. These links can be one-way or two-way. If they are one-way, from site A to site B, then site B will generally pay a royalty or other fee to site A. Where traffic moves both ways, from A to B and from B to A, it will be more usual for no money to change hands, although there may be a payment if more traffic flows from one site to the other. Legal issues also exist in relation to hyperlinks. In addition, companies such as lastminute.com have advertised their online business extensively using conventional media, such as billboards and magazines.

Consolidating your brand and making it work

Having established your brand, the next challenge is to keep customers happy when they get there and to make them keep coming back to do business. It was this that prompted the merger between America On Line (AOL) and Time Warner. AOL is the world's largest ISP, and Time Warner is one of the biggest media content providers in the world, boasting household names such as CNN, Compuserve and *Time* magazine. AOL brings the customers and Time Warner brings the content. In internet terms they are a golden brand, a corporate version of Brad Pitt and Jennifer Aniston. And given that 2 + 2 = 5, it's easy to see why shares rocketed when the merger was announced.

On the internet there is no SW1 postcode or Rodeo Drive address. The status of a site and its brand will depend on its profile, and its ability to induce people to visit it, to trade on it, and return to trade again. The recent high-profile collapse of Boo.com may provide a cautionary tale in relation to internet branding. Launched in a blaze of publicity, and with a cumulative total of almost $120 million in funding, Boo.com was a UK-based internet retailer specialising in youth fashion. For all the hype with Boo.com, it was at this point that their plan began to unwind. Having whetted the appetite of the public for shopping online, they failed to convert publicity into sales. Within six months of the site going live, the liquidators had been brought in. Net revenues for the quarter to end January 2000 had only been $680,000 and the value of the liquidated assets was only $743,400. Some $25 million had been spent mainly on advertising.

Numerous possible reasons for this failure have been cited; it was probably a combination of them all. Firstly, Boo.com failed to adequately cater for the needs of its users in the technology it employed. Customers were subjected to a shopping experience which was, arguably, even less enjoyable than physically going shopping. The system was cumbersome, slow and unable to cope with the pressure put on it. While Boo.com had obtained a great profile, they had failed to back it up with sales.

People would know the name, they might even have a look, but they wouldn't buy. Also, many customers bought once but didn't come back. Almost all businesses rely on repeat business from loyal customers, but on the internet it seems to be even more important than in traditional spheres, so much so that it has spawned the concept of stickability – the number of customers who keep coming back. It is much easier to click on to another site than to drag yourself to another shop. Internet customers seem less willing to accept bad service and poor facilities: one strike and you may well be out, along with your brand.

It has also been argued that Boo.com was before its time; it has been well documented that business-to-consumer (B2C) companies have struggled rather more than business-to-business (B2B) companies. As internet access widens and consumer confidence increases, B2C businesses are certainly becoming more viable. Another reason for the failure of Boo.com may have been that the attractiveness of the concept was overplayed. Just because you can sell clothes over the internet does not mean that it is a good idea.

Some markets lend themselves to internet business far better than others. More people enjoy clothes shopping than buying groceries or household appliances. In particular, research by consultants McKinsey has shown that the more fragmented a market, the more suited it is to forming an internet business. With general shopping, most people find it easy to walk to the shops, assess the quality and value of goods, and make purchases. Boo.com can be contrasted with Build.com, an internet portal established in 1994 to serve the building and home improvement market. Build.com brings together buyers and sellers from all over the United States and beyond, and allows them to deal directly with each other. It allows customers the opportunity to decrease the cost of goods and services supplied to them by bringing together competing suppliers. From the suppliers perspective, they can reach into markets which were previously impenetrable. Build.com has therefore built a market where one previously did not exist; the possibility of establishing a market and a brand such as this has only been possible by the internet. This is undoubtedly one of the most compelling parts of the Build.com business models.

Internet brands are themselves now subject to attack by unauthorised users, known as cybersquatting or domain name hijacking. Established legal principles for brand protection do not quite fit this situation. If someone is just squatting on a name, then arguably they will not actually be doing an act in the course of trade or making a

business representation, which are requirements of trademark infringement and passing off. However, some courts have been able to
come up with lateral and creative thinking to stop cybersquatters.

Usefully, sometimes they have also been prepared to grant
immediate orders to give protection against cybersquatters, even
though there has not yet been a full trial. If an early order can be
obtained comparatively quickly and cheaply, it is likely the matter
will be resolved there and then, as the cybersquatter is unlikely to
want to press matters further. That said, pursuing the matter will still
involve time, legal costs and a court hearing with little chance of
recovering any costs from the other side – but the total cost is almost
definitely less than what the cybersquatter is seeking.

Lateral thinking

*One important example of lateral thinking is the decision of the English
Court of Appeal in* British Telecommunications plc v. One in a Million
*(Court of Appeal, Civil Division, 23 July 1998) on an interlocutory appli-
cation (before full trial) which held that the registering of a domain name,
with no intention to use it and the intention to seek payment in return for
transfer, was possessing an instrument of fraud which could be passing off
and in breach of section 10(3) Trade Marks Act 1994.*

*However, in an application for summary judgement (early judgement on
the basis that the holder of the domain name did not have a case), a judge
refused to give French Connection judgement in respect of fcuk.com. The
domain name had been registered just after a high-profile advertising
campaign had been launched, but French Connection had previously
registered FCUK as a trademark and it had previously been used in
advertising campaigns. The judge held that there was no evidence that
'fcuk' was synonymous with French Connection (French Connection Ltd v.
Antony Toolseram Sutton, High Court, Chancery Division, 3 December
1999).*

*Difficulties have also been encountered in the US, where Avery Dennison
unsuccessfully tried to rely on the Federal Trade Marks Dilution Act 1995.*

The US has, however, recently introduced the Anti-Cybersquatting Con-
sumer Protection Act, which covers registering, trafficking or using a
domain name that is confusingly similar to or dilutes a trademark which is
distinctive or famous at the time of registration of the domain name, when
the domain name is registered in bad faith or with an intent to profit. Also,
if the owner cannot be found within the jurisdiction (Virginia in the case of
Avery Dennison) – a common difficulty with the global nature of the
internet – then direct action may be taken against the domain name
itself.

The situation has been made even more difficult because different countries have different laws, people have different rights in different countries and because judgements of courts in one country may not be recognised by courts in other countries, depending on the circumstances. The first movement to address this situation came early in the piece and it came from outside the legal system. Network Solutions Inc (NSI) is the US body responsible for administering the .com domain name. Because of the difficulties which arose with the growth of the internet, NSI introduced a cybersquatting policy in early 1996. This required an applicant to confirm they were entitled to the domain name, they would use it in good faith and they would not infringe any one else's trademark rights in any country.

The policy was very pro trademark owners and did not address the issue of legitimate coexisting rights. It also stated that the domain name would be suspended pending resolution of any legal disputes regarding entitlement. However, this did not take any actual steps towards resolving the basic problem. NSI were made further aware of the importance of this whole issue when Harrods, concerned at the registration of harrods.com commenced proceedings in the English High Court against NSI as well as the cybersquatter. This raised questions about whether this court could rule against NSI, but NSI in fact consented to abide by the decision of the court (*Harrods v. UK Network Services Limited and Others*, High Court, Chancery Division, 9 December 1996).

With the increased growth of the internet, its management was contracted out from the US government to the Internet Corporation for Assigned Names and Numbers (ICANN). ICANN introduced the Uniform Domain Name Dispute Resolution Policy in 1999. Key features of this policy are that when applying for a domain name, the applicant must confirm that the registration will not be in breach of the rights of a third party, that it is not registered for an unlawful purpose and that it is not knowingly used in breach of laws.

The registrant must submit to arbitration if a complainant alleges that a domain name is the same or confusingly similar to a trademark owned by the complainant, that the domain name owner has no legitimate interest in the domain name and that the domain name was not registered and is not used in good faith.

- *Indications of bad faith*: an intent to profit through speculation, a desire to prevent the owner of a trademark having a corresponding domain name, an intent to disrupt others' business, or an intent to pass off.
- *Indications of good faith*: use of the domain name before the dispute arises, use of own name (which has led to one Australian man changing his name to Mr Oxford University), non-commercial or fair use without any intent to pass off or tarnish another's reputation or trademark.

If these requirements are all satisfied, it may be ordered that the domain name be transferred. It is possible for a dispute to be referred to court before or within 10 days after this administration procedure. If this is done, no action will be taken until the court action is at an end.

The ICANN policy has been adopted by all accredited .com domain name registrars, including NSI (which also controls the .net and .org suffixes), and by some registrars for country codes. However, Nominet, which administers the .co.uk suffixes, has not adopted the ICANN policy. Nominet has its own policy, which is really only to encourage the parties to resolve the matter through mediation, although it may cancel or suspend the registration. Nominet has stated that it considers the UK courts to be the appropriate forum for resolving disputes. It is possible that this may deter people from using .co.uk. The widespread adoption of the ICANN policy is an encouraging sign and it is hoped the policy will be adopted even more widely.

WIPO is the World Intellectual Property Organisation. ICANN has approved the WIPO Arbitration and Mediation Centre, the National Arbitration Forum and Disputes.org as dispute resolution service providers under the policy. In addition, if disputes are dealt with under the ICANN policy, it avoids the difficult issue of whether any national court is in fact able to rule on a dispute (even if they have the appropriate national law) and then ensure that its rulings are followed. The WIPO avenue has already been successfully used by the World Wrestling Foundation, actor Julia Roberts and author Jeannette Winterson. The procedure is fairly straightforward and involves filing a written complaint with WIPO.

While these systems recognise and try to deal with the fact that cybersquatting may occur, they do not address the question of two people owning the same trademark or having built up substantial and legitimate reputations which are worthy of protection, in different countries. This is where traditional brand protection mechanisms, such as registration of trademarks, continue to be relevant.

CONCLUSION

The internet is not the death knell of brands, it is the catalyst for creating new internet brands. These new brands will need to generate consumer loyalty even more than traditional brands, as profit will be generated by continual repeat visits rather than single intermittent purchases. The wish to buy two- and three-letter domain names highlights the value of short memorable names in a world of instantaneous communication.

About the Authors

Clive Callow has had widespread experience in financial business news, starting as an editorial assistant in the newsroom of the *Financial Times* in the 1960s. After working for a US publication specialising in the petroleum industry, he joined the *Times*, where he covered the early days of the North Sea oil search. His book, *Power from the Sea*, remains one of the best early accounts of this major UK industrial enterprise. Subsequently he became an oil analyst, helping to form the London Oil Analysts Group. Clive Callow is joint editor of *Professional Investor* and an associate of KBR.

John Goodchild is joint editor of *Professional Investor* and has contributed articles on investment theory and practice to numerous magazines. He co-edited with Paul Hewitt a collection of essays on the Unlisted Securities Market, published by the IIMR (now UKSIP). In 2000 he and Clive Callow edited *Double Takes*, which was published by John Wiley & Sons Ltd. Originally an analyst with Mullens & Co., John Goodchild is now an associate with KBR, the London stockbrokers.

Jonathan Knowles is a leading thinker and practitioner of corporate and service branding, and a regular speaker at conferences and business schools on the role of branding in business strategy. Formerly head of consulting at Wolff Olins, Europe's foremost brand consultancy, he began his career at the Bank of England, where he spent six years in the international and banking supervisory areas. He left in 1991 to do an MBA at INSEAD then worked for three years at the value-based strategy consultants Marakon Associates. He is currently Managing Director of Type 2 Consulting and is based in New York.

Shonaig Macpherson heads McGrigor Donald's intellectual property unit, which deals with intellectual property and information technology matters for a wide range of clients. The technology unit advises on fundraising and large corporate transactions. She specialises in the protection and exploitation of intellectual property rights, and advises on all aspects of R&D, joint venture, licensing and fundraising. Shonaig is company secretary of the Scottish Biomedical Research Trust, a member of the Licensing Executive Society, the Society for Computers and Law, and the International Trade Marks Association. In 1997 she became a visiting professor of Heriot-Watt University.

Lucinda Spicer leads specialist valuation services for PricewaterhouseCoopers (PwC) in the UK. Her wide professional experience covers commercial and tax-based valuations, transaction-structuring advice, and UK and international tax consulting. Lucinda is currently managing PwC's development of techniques in determining the cost of capital in complex valuation situations. She has a particular interest in the assessment of business risk, in the measurement of the contribution that intellectual property makes to business in the hi-tech and consumer products sectors, and in the valuation and funding of highly leveraged companies.

Caroline Woodward is a director in the Corporate Value Consulting practice of PricewaterhouseCoopers (PwC) in London. She has over thirteen years' experience of business and intangible asset valuation for a variety of purposes. Caroline spent over seven years with PwC in Central and Eastern Europe carrying out valuations for privatisations and for more traditional M&A situations. Her expertise lies in the consumer and industrial products sector, with particular emphasis on pharmaceuticals. She directs assignments for business and share valuation for transactions and for restructuring purposes and the valuation of intangible assets for financial reporting purposes.

Index